Managing Software Development with Trac and Subversion

Simple project management for software development

David J Murphy

BIRMINGHAM - MUMBAI

Managing Software Development with Trac and Subversion

First published: December 2007

Production Reference: 1071207

Published by Packt Publishing Ltd.
32 Lincoln Road
Olton
Birmingham, B27 6PA, UK.

ISBN 978-1-847191-66-3

www.packtpub.com

Cover Image by Karl Moore (karl.moore@ukonline.co.uk)

Credits

Author

David J Murphy

Reviewers

Andy Allan

Patrick Ben Koetter

Sarah George

Senior Acquisition Editor

David Barnes

Development Editor

Mithil Kulkarni

Technical Editor

Akshara Aware

Editorial Team Leader

Mithil Kulkarni

Project Manager

Abhijeet Deobhakta

Project Coordinator

Patricia Weir

Sagara Naik

Indexer

Hemangini Bari

Proofreader

Chris Smith

Production Coordinator

Shantanu Zagade

Cover Designer

Shantanu Zagade

About the Author

David J Murphy has worked in IT since 1996 and has focused on development since 1998. He works for Canonical Ltd. as a Software Developer, and prior to this he was a Product Specialist with Computer Sciences Corporation. He is a strong advocate of free and open-source software, and has contributed to two Linux books. He has also written several articles for magazines and the Internet.

He lives in Cumbria, UK with his wife, two children, a dog, and numerous cats.

His personal website is http://schwuk.com.

I dedicate this book to my wife Suzanne, and our children Alexandra and Tristan.

About One of the Reviewer

Patrick Ben Koetter is the Chief Technologist for state of mind, Partnerschaft Koetter, Schmidt & Schosser, a systems integrator, and was Information Architect at the Ludwig-Maximilians Universität in Munich, Germany. He has written articles for Germany's c't magazine, *Linuxmagazin,* and other magazines as well. Patrick is co-author of *The Book of Postfix.* As a consultant and trainer, Patrick regularly teaches classes on email, anti-virus, and spam measurements and application-level Web interfaces. He has given talks at many conferences on these and similiar topics.

Table of Contents

Preface

Software development is not just about writing code - we need to manage the entire process.

This book looks at that process, how it can be managed, and how Trac and Subversion can help us achieve this. It combines theory with practical knowledge and experience that most developers will relate to.

Trac is an open-source, web-based project management and bug-tracking tool. Trac is an enhanced wiki and issue-tracking system for software development projects. Trac uses a minimalistic approach to web-based software project management. Trac is written in the Python programming language. In computing, Subversion (SVN) is a version control system (VCS). It allows users to keep track of changes made to any type of electronic data, typically source code, web pages, or design documents.

What This Book Covers

Chapter 1 covers the basics of task management and how these apply to software development. It also looks into another important skill needed for managing projects—communication—and discusses the problems faced during software development and how they can be solved.

Chapter 2 introduces the various applications used for implementing the solution discussed in the chapter. Trac and Subversion are the main parts of the solution, but by no means the only ones.

Chapter 3 along with the appendices shows how to install these applications on Microsoft Windows or Linux.

Chapter 4 discusses how to create and use documentation using Trac.

Chapter 5 brings us back to the topic of task management and we again focus on Trac and how it helps us with this.

Chapter 6 explores the basics of using Subversion and looks at how it integrates with Trac.

Chapter 7 shows how Trac and Subversion can be used together to manage the the two most frequent events in the development cycle of an application—fixing a bug and implementing a new feature.

Appendix A covers detailed, step by step instructions for installing Subversion on your system, and cover Microsoft Windows and Linux.

Appendix B covers detailed, step by step instructions for installing the Apache web server on your system, and covers Microsoft Windows and Linux

Appendix C covers detailed, step by step instructions for installing the Apache web server on your system, and covers Microsoft Windows and Linux

Who is This Book for

This book is for developers of all calibres, and particularly those that lead teams or projects, especially if they have recently moved into the role or are simply looking for a "better way".

Conventions

In this book, you will find a number of styles of text that distinguish between different kinds of information. Here are some examples of these styles, and an explanation of their meaning.

There are three styles for code. Code words in text are shown as follows: "The -m "Initial repository structure" specifies a log message for the action(s) we are performing—creating folders in this fashion is actually checking in the changes directly on the server."

A block of code will be set as follows:

```
[ticket]
default_component =
default_milestone =
default_priority = major
```

When we wish to draw your attention to a particular part of a code block, the relevant lines or items will be made bold:

```
Password for 'jdoe':
Authentication realm: <http://projects.example.com:80> Subversion
Repositories
Username: user@example.com
Password for 'user@example.com':
Path: sandbox
```

Any command-line input and output is written as follows:

```
# svn mkdir http://servername/svn/sandbox/trunk
              http://servername/svn/sandbox/tags
              http://servername/svn/sandbox/branches
              -m "Initial repository structure"
```

New terms and **important words** are introduced in a bold-type font. Words that you see on the screen, in menus or dialog boxes for example, appear in our text like this: "clicking the **Next** button moves you to the next screen".

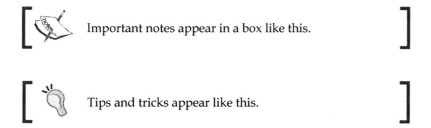

Important notes appear in a box like this.

Tips and tricks appear like this.

Reader Feedback

Feedback from our readers is always welcome. Let us know what you think about this book, what you liked or may have disliked. Reader feedback is important for us to develop titles that you really get the most out of.

To send us general feedback, simply drop an email to feedback@packtpub.com, making sure to mention the book title in the subject of your message.

If there is a book that you need and would like to see us publish, please send us a note in the **SUGGEST A TITLE** form on www.packtpub.com or email suggest@packtpub.com.

If there is a topic that you have expertise in and you are interested in either writing or contributing to a book, see our author guide on www.packtpub.com/authors.

Customer Support

Now that you are the proud owner of a Packt book, we have a number of things to help you to get the most from your purchase.

Errata

Although we have taken every care to ensure the accuracy of our contents, mistakes do happen. If you find a mistake in one of our books—maybe a mistake in text or code—we would be grateful if you would report this to us. By doing this you can save other readers from frustration, and help to improve subsequent versions of this book. If you find any errata, report them by visiting http://www.packtpub.com/support, selecting your book, clicking on the **Submit Errata** link, and entering the details of your errata. Once your errata are verified, your submission will be accepted and the errata added to the list of existing errata. The existing errata can be viewed by selecting your title from http://www.packtpub.com/support.

Questions

You can contact us at questions@packtpub.com if you are having a problem with some aspect of the book, and we will do our best to address it.

1
Understanding the Problem

Developing software can be compared to an organic process like planting a garden. With the right conditions, something will grow, but it may not be what we want or indeed grow the way we want it. We might end up with a garden of roses or a jungle of weeds. Any experienced gardener will tell us that what our garden needs most is planning and tending, and the same is true for software development.

Of course, we can just start writing the code and we will get something — maybe even something that works! — but if we invest a little time and effort in planning before we write a single line, and in ensuring we tend the code we write, then we are far more likely to achieve an end result that bears some resemblance to our initial vision.

We need to manage our software development.

Before we dive deep into knowing what managing software development is, we need to understand that, in essence, it is just a specific form of 'project management' — two words that send most developers running for the hills! A lot has been written about project management and the various styles and techniques thereof, which to the initiated make it live up to its common portrayal as a highly confusing and specialized field. The truth is that *usable* project management is within our grasp, and we don't need expensive software or a certification to be able to put it into practice. In essence it exercises two distinct, yet complementary skills — task management and communication.

Therefore, I would like you to take a lengthy look at project management and in particular how it applies to software development.

Task Management

This is one of those things that is easy to say, but not as easy to do—especially for a novice. While we do need to keep a view of the overall project, a project is nothing more than a collection of tasks, and it is the management of these tasks that will help us to successfully complete our project. To help us to understand task management better we will not look at it as a whole, but rather as the sum of its parts. By looking at the specific activities involved in managing tasks it will become clear that it is an iterative process that is driven by logic—something we as developers are meant to be good at! Demonstrating with the help of an example is the easiest way to learn so let us consider a hypothetical project to build a wall for our garden.

Wait, we are supposed to be developers. If we are to remain true to our stereotypes then we would avoid manual labor and possibly even leaving the office. Instead we would just hire a contractor to build the wall for us and get back to writing code. However, even if we do take this approach, does not prevent us from viewing it as a project. Although our contractor will do most of the work for us, we still need to find good contractors, hire them, schedule the work, and pay them. Although it is much easier than the example that follows, we still have a collection of related tasks, and as such is considered a project.

Having decided to defy convention and build the wall ourselves, let's look at the activities that allow us to manage our tasks and complete our project:

- **Task Determination**: Obviously we need tasks to manage, and although our first instinct may be to determine every single possible task at the outset, we need to remember that this is an iterative process so tasks can (and will) be added, changed, or removed later on. We will also find that we do not have to think too hard to determine our tasks—as the saying goes "one thing leads to another"; likewise as one task comes to mind others will become apparent.

- **Dependency Management**: Some tasks can be completed in isolation; others may have prerequisites—other tasks that need to be fulfilled before they can be started. As with determining our tasks, we will find that the dependencies come naturally.

- **Resource Management**: Resources can cover a number of things; unless we have a specific requirement to cater for, it is simpler, and therefore easier, to limit our scope to people. We may only have one resource (ourselves) to worry about or we may have a team, but as long as we include this activity when managing our tasks then we will always be prepared if we need to manage additional resources later.

- **Scheduling**: Once these activities have been completed for the first time (or iteration) we can look at understanding and deciding when a given task needs to be completed. A simple due date will suffice, although we can include a start date if we desire.

- **Task Execution**: Getting it done. There is no point managing our tasks and projects if we never complete them!

- **Reviewing**: As with task execution above, reviewing is an essential part of task management. Just marking a task as completed is part of the reviewing process, but when doing so we can take the opportunity to see how our progress is affecting the list. Are we behind schedule? Has the task we have just completed brought new tasks or dependencies to mind? Always take time to review your tasks, even if doing so is a task in itself.

By now project management practitioners will be complaining about the exclusion of priorities and timescales for tasks, but including these is purely down to your personal preference.

With regards to priorities, if we choose to incorporate them we need a method of representing the priority of a given task. While assigning numerical or alphabetical labels is common practice, it is far easier and more accessible to think of them simply in terms of low, normal (or medium), and high. As part of task determination and dependency management activities, it will also be apparent which tasks are of a higher or lower priority compared to others. A simple rule of thumb would be that if a task is of high priority then, it will most likely have a number of dependencies and hence top our task list.

As for timescales, these will either be so fine grained (task a will take x minutes) or broad (1 week to complete three dependent tasks) that they will just make things complicated for us. If the due dates we choose during task determination are insufficient for our planning purposes then we need to understand why that is before we start incorporating timescales into our task management process.

Getting back to our example of building a wall, let's have a look at the activities in action.

We know we want to build a wall, which is our project goal. The first obvious activity is to decide where we want to build the wall, so we have determined the task of "Choose Location". We also need to prepare the site so "Clear Location" and "Lay Foundation" can be included. Of course for the foundation we need "Dig Foundation". For building the wall we need materials — "Buy Materials", which leads us to "Price Materials" and "Arrange Delivery Date" (if we are not picking them up ourselves). Our site is prepared, and we have our materials so we can now think about "Laying Bricks", which leads to both "Mixing Mortar" and "Cleaning Up".

We have determined ten tasks that need to be completed to achieve our goal from a simple objective. Next we need to think about dependencies — choosing and clearing the location can be carried out while we price and buy the materials, but digging the foundation and mixing the mortar need to be completed before we lay any bricks, and of course we also need the materials before we mix the mortar or lay the bricks.

Managing resources does not require too much effort for this project as we will be doing all the work ourselves, but we may choose our partner to take care of purchasing the materials or a friend may offer to help out with the actual labor, so we must not skip this step.

Now can we begin to schedule the work. The independent tasks such as choosing and preparing the location can be scheduled as we desire. For the other tasks though, we may not be able to make those decisions yet. We may have a rough idea of when we want the wall completed, and if a friend has offered to help then we will know when they are available, but until we have arranged the delivery of the materials we cannot confirm when we will build the wall.

No that we have figured all our tasks, we can focus on task execution — in this case purchasing the materials and arranging their delivery.

Once these have been completed we can go back and review our tasks. We can now mark some as complete, while others will now need to be scheduled. We may even think of more tasks that could be included.

Following this simple example, we can see that with least efforts we now know exactly what tasks we need to do and when we need to do them, so that we can concentrate on getting them done.

Communication

A perfectly crafted task list is useless if you don't communicate it. Continuing with the above example, we need to communicate with the material supplier so that we can schedule other tasks, and we may need to communicate with our friend so they know what they are supposed to do and when. We may also need to communicate with our neighbors so that they are aware of our building work. Communication naturally involves the review activity, because while talking to our friend we can adjust our task list if they can't make it on a certain day, or while informing the neighbors of our plans additional tasks — such as obtaining planning permission — may become apparent.

Exercising task management and communication provides us with enough to manage most projects, without a Gantt chart in sight!

Project Management for Software Development

We have seen that effective project management consists of managing tasks and maintaining communication. We need to apply this fundamental approach to software development as well. While there are additional considerations, as there are with any other special field, it is the core capabilities of determining what needs to be done and communicating with all interested parties (i.e. team members and customers) that distinguish the successful projects from the unsuccessful ones. The good news is that due to the nature of software development, and the environment in which it is performed, both of these will be much easier that the actual development itself.

The determination of tasks will be as natural a process as it was in our example of building a wall. There are obvious activities that need to be carried out and they will have an obvious sequence in which they need to be completed. Unless we are running an open-source project where developers can come and go, our resources need to be clearly defined (even if it is just ourselves!). Scheduling will be driven by the deadlines we have been set, have agreed to, or have set for ourselves.

Since we are working on, and with, computers we have two ready methods of communication available to us—email and the web browser. The former allows us to participate in a two way dialog with others, while the latter was designed for disseminating information—with the right infrastructure of course.

With the basics of project management covered, we need to consider additional features that benefit software development:

- **Documentation**: For the developers this could take the form of requirements, best practices, or API documentation. For the users we have installation, usage, and troubleshooting guides as well as the ever-present Frequently Asked Questions (FAQ).

- **Roadmaps**: Software development is rarely a single project with a set goal. More often the software itself goes through a series of versions or releases, which can be translated to a series of connected projects (for each release) or an open-ended one. Roadmaps allow us to share—communicate—these plans with both our developers and users.

- **Error Reports**: No software is perfect—no matter how much its developer likes to claims it is! —and so we need a mechanism for our testers and users to report faults and errors to us so that they can be managed. Capturing error reports is not the end result though. We must also ensure that they are managed so they can be resolved to both our and the reporter's satisfaction.

- **Requirements**: These could come directly from a user in the form of a feature request, or we could determine that a particular error report requires us to change our software. Irrespective of how we receive or capture them, they need to be managed in the same manner as error reports.

- **Revision Control**: Revision control allows us to store all files related to a particular software development project. In addition to storing the files, it also stores versions of each file, so that changes can be tracked. This allows us to see who has done what with each file, and if necessary, roll back (reverse) those changes. A well-managed software project has the ability to have the code reviewed at any point during its life cycle. Whether we are checking for bugs in the currently released version while a new one is being actively developed, or re-creating a previous version to see why something was changed, revision control is a mainstay of software development these days, which no serious project is without, especially when development is handled by a team, particularly a geographically distributed one.

- **Releases**: To allow our software to be used we need to release it—either as an installation package or a bundle of files—and we need to provide access to those releases.

Providing these features is only part of the battle—for them to really add value to our development process they need to be implemented as a cohesive whole. If documentation is in one system, error reports are in another, and tasks in yet another then that solution is unwieldy and we will resist using it. Stick them together in a system that remains awkward to use and we will still resist using it. Give us a "development support system" that ties these elements together in an unobtrusive way that allows us to focus on what we really care about—developing software and writing code—and we have something that will make our lives easier.

It is not just about providing a solution for the developers though; it is also about the way that they use it. If the system is used in a prescribed way and consistently by all, then we have a process for managing software development.

Managing Software Development

As we have seen, managing software development goes beyond basic project management, but we can still see the basics: what needs to be done. We have just looked at the additional requirements for software development, and now we will see how this book will help us address them.

Keep Ourselves Organized

Things are much easier to find if we know where to look for them, whether we are talking about car keys or source code. If we lay the foundations, as we did for our wall, before we write a single line of code, then our project has a better chance of succeeding. As with task determination we don't need to plan for every eventuality, we just need to make sure that the obvious basics are covered. We need to consider things as follows:

How Our Project is Laid Out on the File System

This would include the following:

- How we handle third-party code
- Coding style
- How we are going to name our files
- What we are going to store in our revision control
- When (or how often) we are going to put our changes into revision control
- What we need to be able to develop e.g. compilers, IDEs, etc.

All these need to be documented — another word that can send developers running for the hills! This may seem like a significant amount of work to do before we even think about our first line of code, but it will save us time in the long run. In addition, once we have done this once, we will be able to reuse some or all of these details for other projects to get a head start next time.

Developers Are Users Too

We need to turn our preparation work into a best-practices guide for our developers. They are the users of our system, and they need a user guide to allow them to use it as we intend it to be used. Investing the time in preparing the system and its documentation means that more time can be spent on actual development. By providing our developers, or rather users, with clearly defined standards and practices we remove all ambiguity and reduce friction that could delay our project.

The principle we applied to task management can also be used here—we don't need to prepare for and document every eventuality, we just need to provide solid enough foundations for our developers to build on. We must seek not to weigh our developers down with unnecessary rules, but rather provide just enough to guide them to maximal productivity.

We will also apply the review activity from task management to our documentation—it needs to evolve with our project, not constrain it. As our developers use our system, things may change to suit the project in question, which is a good thing. Our documentation needs to be a living thing, not a dusty set of rules locked away in a library.

We also need to provide documentation of our software to the users, and ideally this will be written as the software develops. Some projects may be lucky enough to have a dedicated technical author, but even those will benefit from writing the documentation alongside the software. If a dedicated resource for documentation is not available then we will certainly find it easier to write the documentation with the software, not afterwards.

Everything Is a Task

Every aspect of software development, from writing documentation through implementing a new feature and fixing bugs to packaging for a release, needs to be considered as a task. We need to make sure that they are all captured and then processed as outlined earlier in this chapter. If we use tasks correctly then the developers will always know what they personally have left to do, and likewise our project leader will know what is left to be done to reach the next release. By using the task information to create and update our roadmap—a concept we will look at in greater detail later—everyone will always be able to determine where we are going.

Sandboxes Aren't Just for Children

Now that our "development support system" is set up, our developers know how to use it, and our tasks are being managed, we can finally write some code! We can save ourselves a significant amount of effort by developing in isolation. This means keeping our work separate from other developers' work until it is ready—features and bug fixes are developed away from the main code, and only integrated when complete. This means that:

- We are developing against a known base, not a constantly changing one.
- We are responsible for making sure our code integrates with the rest; if another developer integrates their bug fix before we integrate our new feature, the blame can only lie with ourselves if our code doesn't work or we break something the other developer fixed.

Isolating code changes can also allow a single developer to tackle multiple tasks simultaneously.

Small Steps are Better

While we may want to plow through the new feature we are adding in one go, it is much better to take small steps and implement it piece by piece. It means we are less likely to introduce bugs by making sweeping changes, and if we are using our revision control to track every change then we have a much richer history to step back through when required. As with everything there needs to be balance found, and a good rule of thumb is to only store a change in our revision control when that particular change *works*. Then we can move on to the next change with confidence.

Summary

So far we have seen how project management can be pared down to two main activities—task management and communication. We also saw how to practice these in a real situation. Next we looked at the additional requirements that we have for software development projects. Then finally we had a brief look at some of the ideas that make managing software development easier. In the next chapter we will be introduced to software components that we will use to power our "development support system" and learn how in this case the whole is greater than the sum of the parts.

2
Introducing the Solution

Now that we have understood the problems that make managing software development difficult to the uninitiated, and have discussed the methods we are going to use to make our lives easier, it is time to meet the software that is going to enable us to put these methods into practice. In addition to introducing the software packages we will also look at how they work together to provide the overall solution.

An Ensemble Cast

It should be no surprise (especially considering the title of this book!) that Trac and Subversion are the key players in our solution, and they provide a good chunk of the functionality that we need. What may come as a surprise is that for the solution to really meet our needs there needs to be a third player—the Apache web server. There is also a fourth part, WebDAV, which we implement via an Apache module, and hence could be considered to have only a supporting role; but we will see later that it does contribute to the overall solution.

Now we know who the four players in our solution are, let's learn a bit more about them before we learn how they fit, and more importantly work, together.

Subversion

Subversion (`http://subversion.tigris.org/`) is a version control system released under an Apache/BSD-style open-source license.

What is version control?

Version control, also referred to as revision control, source control, or source code management (SCM), is the management of multiple versions of a single item or collection thereof. Commonly used in documentation, engineering, and software development processes, particularly where a team of people are involved, it enables the tracking and retrieval of changes made to an item. Each revision is assigned a (sequential) number and normally associated with the person who makes the change. In its simplest form, each time a document is issued it is assigned the next number in the sequence starting at 1. At a future date an individual could obtain copies of the current and original documents and compare the differences between the two.

Version control systems for the purpose of software development manage all the details of this process for us, even down to identifying the differences between versions for us. Version control is considered essential for modern software development.

Often referred to by the name of its client, svn, Subversion was developed as a replacement for the venerable Concurrent Versions System (CVS) and the majority of commands are the same across both systems, which makes migration easier for existing users.

CVS itself grew from an older versioning system, Revision Control System (RCS). RCS handled individual files, but not whole projects. Although statistically CVS is still widely used, the popularity of Subversion is steadily growing and it has been said that people switch to Subversion just because they want to use Trac! Many high-profile open-source projects including Mono and Ruby on Rails use Subversion for their version control requirements, and Sourceforge (http://sourceforge.net/) provides Subversion in addition to its traditional CVS hosting while Google Code (http://code.google.com/hosting/) uses Subversion exclusively.

Some of the concepts discussed here may be new to those unfamiliar with revision control, but they will be explained in Chapter 7.

Subversion's features include:

- **Feature compatibility with CVS**: As it is intended to be an improved CVS, most of the features are implemented so as to behave similarly to their CVS equivalents.

- **Versioning for folders, renames and properties**: All these features are missing in CVS, which is one of the most common complaints against it. In addition to files and their contents, Subversion provides versioning for folders and support for renaming. It also allows arbitrary metadata ("properties") to be versioned along with any file or directory, which amongst other things provides a mechanism for retaining 'execute' permission flags on files.

- **Atomic commits**: Committing a change, any change, to the subversion repository will not take place unless all aspects of the commit are successful. A given commit may contain changes to multiple files, and revision numbers and logs are assigned to the commit, not individual files.

- **Support for hosting via Apache and WebDAV**: As we will see later Subversion can be hosted behind an Apache web server, which provides additional features like authentication, traffic compression, and basic repository access through a browser.

- **Standalone operation**: It can alternatively be run by itself with no additional software, or tunneled over Secure Shell (SSH) for additional security if the supported basic authentication does not suffice.

- **'Lightweight' branching and tagging**: Actually these are the same thing under Subversion, yet are considered separately for convention's sake. CVS treated these actions differently for performance reasons, but Subversion's efficient copy method removes the need for tagging. Designed to take up a minimal amount of space and time to create.

- **Client/server and layered by design**: Subversion was designed to be client/server from the outset, avoiding some of the maintenance problems that have plagued other systems. From a developer's point of view Subversion is laid out as a set of connected modules with well-defined interfaces, which allow other applications to directly hook into core functionality

- **Bandwidth efficient**: By only sending the differences between versions of a file in both directions whenever possible, bandwidth usage is optimized.

- **Performance depends on the change, not the size of the project**: Making a small change to a large project should take the same amount of time or traffic as making the same change to a smaller one. While this is not a feature exclusive to Subversion, it is not present in all version control systems.

- **Database or filesystem-based repositories**: These can be created using an embedded database engine (so no separate database server is needed), or as a normal flat-file back-end, which uses a custom format.

- **Symbolic links versioning**: UNIX users can place symbolic links under version control. The links are recreated in UNIX working copies, but not in Win32 working copies. Handled correctly where supported (UNIX) and ignored where not (Win32).

- **Efficient binary file support**: Although revision works best with plain text files, binary files can be stored and even compared at a basic level.

- **Parseable output**: The Subversion client is carefully designed to be human readable yet facilitate automation.

- **Localized**: Support for displaying error, informational, and help messages based on the current locale settings.

Subversion is good, but it is not perfect and so may not be suited to every project. Extremely large projects may suffer performance issues, and Subversion does not support off-line or disconnected operation. However, its power and flexibility make it well suited to meet the requirements of most developers.

As was stated in the preface, this book is not intended to be an extensive reference to Subversion. There are already numerous titles available that look in depth at the software. However, we shouldn't run off to the bookstore just yet as everything we need to know to be able to implement and operate the solution presented here is contained in this book.

Trac

While all the parts of our solution are considered equally important, the truth is that without Trac this solution, and this book, would not exist!

Trac is an open-source project created and directed by the developers at Edgewall Software (http://www.edgewall.org). They are a community of software developers who collaborate on a number of open-source projects, all of which share the common theme of being based on the Python programming language (http://www.python.org/). Trac won the UK Linux & Open Source Award for Best Linux OSS Developer Tool in 2006.

Perhaps the best way to describe Trac is as a "wiki on steroids" — the developers themselves describe it as an "enhanced wiki and issue tracking system".

What on earth is a wiki?

A wiki, originally referred to as a WikiWikiWeb, is a web application that allows visitors to create and modify its content. The most famous example of a wiki in action is Wikipedia (`http://wikipedia.org`), which is a collaboratively edited encyclopedia.

A wiki enables documents to be written—usually in a markup language intended to be easier to learn and use than HTML—using a web browser. Any given page in a wiki is known singularly as a "wiki page", while the entire body of pages, is "the wiki"; in effect, a wiki is actually a very simple, easy-to-use user-maintained database for storing and retrieving information.

One defining characteristic of a wiki is the way individual wiki pages link to each other, and even to pages that do not (yet) exist. These links are created automatically by the wiki software dependent on the particular markup for that wiki. The most common method for indicating a link to another wiki page is to use a CamelCase word—that is two words mashed together and Title Cased—however, other methods do exist.

It is, however, more than just a wiki. The following section introduces its main features.

Wiki

The wiki within Trac is used for all text and documentation throughout the application, including its own user documentation. Since it is a wiki, no structure is enforced and we are left to organize (and reorganize) our information as we see fit. The wiki engine is extensible by way of macros and processors to provide additional functionality not contained in Trac. Attachments are also supported, but unfortunately images need to be hosted externally to Trac for the best results. There are ways around this, but they are not perfect.

The wiki component also has version control built right in—each saved edit of a page results in a stored copy of that page that we can browse or revert to at any time.

Tickets

The Trac ticket system provides simple but effective issue tracking within our project. Combined with the roadmap, tickets provide the core project management elements of Trac, in which tickets are used to track project tasks, feature requests, bug reports, and software support issues.

Each issue is assigned to a person who takes responsibility for either resolving it or reassigning it to another person. All aspects of the ticket can be edited and/or amended while it is active, but keeping with the version control theme all changes are tracked within a ticket so we can see what was changed and by whom.

Fields

Each ticket contains the following properties:

- **Reporter**: The name or (more likely) email address of the person who created the ticket.
- **Type**: The nature of the ticket (e.g. reporting a defect or requesting an enhancement).
- **Component**: The project module this ticket concerns.
- **Version**: The version of the project that this ticket is associated with.
- **Keywords**: Keywords that a ticket is marked with. Useful for searching and report generation.
- **Priority**: The importance of this ticket.
- **Milestone**: The release this ticket needs to be completed for.
- **Owner**: Person responsible for progressing the issue.
- **Cc**: A comma-separated list of other users or email addresses to notify. Note that this does not imply responsibility or any other policy.
- **Resolution**: Summarizes why ticket was closed.
- **Status**: The current status of the ticket.
- **Summary**: A brief description of the issue.
- **Description**: The body of the ticket, detailing what the ticket has been created for.

Roadmap

An extension of the tickets module, the roadmap provides a view of the ticket system that aids in planning and managing the future development of the project. The roadmap lists future milestones against which tickets can be linked. The roadmap then provides summaries of tickets and their statuses so that progress can be tracked.

Milestones can also be given descriptions (again using the wiki engine) and target dates.

Subversion Repository Browser

The Subversion Repository Browser provides access through our web browser to the subversion repository and the folders and files contained therein. We can navigate both through the project file structure and through its revision history. It can also provide detailed information on revisions as a whole, rather than specific files, and will display differences between revisions.

Timeline

If the roadmap tells us where we are going and tickets tell us how to get there, then the timeline tells us where we have been. It provides us with a chronological view of the activity within the project as a single report. All Trac events that have occurred are listed in order of occurrence, including a brief description of each event and where applicable, the person responsible for the change.

The following kinds of events are listed:

- **Wiki page events**: Creation and changes
- **Ticket events**: Creation and resolution/closing (and optionally other changes)
- **Source code changes**: Repository check-ins
- **Milestone**: Milestone completed

Following the wiki style, each event provides a hyperlink to the specific event concerned. The report is also available as an RSS feed.

As we can see Trac is a extremely powerful and flexible piece of software, but it is one that tries hard not to be too constraining so that it can be adapted to the way that we work rather than forcing us into its way of thinking.

Apache Web Server

The Apache web server (http://httpd.apache.org/) is an open-source web server that runs on UNIX-style systems, Microsoft Windows, and other operating platforms, and is released under the Apache license. It is commonly — but incorrectly — referred to just as Apache, and we will do so here for the sake of brevity. It is by far the most popular web server on the Internet, and is often the yardstick by which other web servers are measured.

It provides many, many features, the majority of which we are going to ignore for the purposes of implementing our solution. However one feature it provides is essential to our needs.

Authentication

As we are going to be using Apache to provide access to Trac and Subversion, then it makes sense to centralize our authentication here instead of maintaining multiple systems.

There are many titles are already dedicated to documenting Apache and its configuration, so, as for Subversion, this book will only provide us with the information we need to implement and use it for our needs.

WebDAV

Although the WebDAV implementation we are going to use is provided by Apache and could have been included in the list above, it is listed separately because it is not required for core functionality; but we are going to use it to provide additional features for our solution that we do not get with a straight Trac and Subversion combo.

WebDAV is an abbreviation of Web-based Distributed Authoring and Versioning, which refers to both an IETF working group and the set of extensions to the HTTP protocol that the group defined, which allows users to collaboratively edit and manage files on remote web servers. Its aim is to provide the functionality to create and manage documents on a web server. The obvious use for this is for authoring and publishing the documents that a web server serves, but it can also be utilized for general web-based file storage that is accessible from anywhere. Support for WebDAV is provided by most modern operating systems, and with the right client and a fast network it can be almost as easy to use files on a WebDAV server as those stored in local directories.

Our use for WebDAV is to:

- Provide access to 'publish' releases and supporting files for download
- Provide controlled access to non-wiki documents
- Provide a publishing mechanism for images to be included in wiki pages without using attachments

Since we are already using Apache to provide authentication for Trac and Subversion, we can extend that to provide access control to our WebDAV files as well.

How It All Fits Together

We have our four parts—Trac, Subversion, Apache, and WebDAV. So how do they fit together?

Although we have four parts, we only end up with a two-tiered system. We will be using Apache to provide access and authentication to Trac, Subversion, and WebDAV. This relationship can be seen in the following figure.

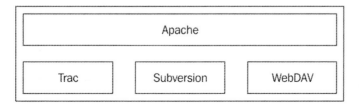

Since all these components are linked and we depend on Apache to access them, we are going to use a single machine to host them all. This will become our server—the hub of our development process.

Summary

So we have looked at what we are going to use, and discussed why these choices lend themselves well to our solution for managing software development. We are using Trac for managing the development process, Subversion to manage our source code, WebDav for managing access to files, and Apache to tie them all together.

In the next chapter we will see how to install and configure them all on two of the most popular platforms: Linux and Microsoft Windows.

3

Laying the Foundations

In this chapter we will cover installing the server components of our framework on the platform of our choice. Although there are numerous platforms that our framework will run on, you will find only specific instructions here for Linux and Microsoft Windows. However, the configuration details can be used on any platform that can run the components.

Which Platform?

Our choice of platform may be influenced by company policy, personal preference, or simply what we have to hand in terms of hardware, software, and experience. Although the installation instructions differ between each platform, there should be no discernible difference in the end result.

As we will see shortly, there can be a significant discrepancy between the latest available version of a component and the version available for our platform. However, our choice of platform should not be made simply because it has the latest versions available. Unless our server is going to remain completely isolated (highly unlikely) we need to consider how it will fit with the rest of our network—a decision we may not have control over. Other considerations include licensing. Although the components concerned are available under a free (or equivalent) software license, the underlying operating system may have its own license restrictions.

Linux

If we have the necessary skills available to operate a Linux server (or the desire to learn), then it provides an almost ideal platform for our server. Because it is free, both in terms of software and licensing, dependent on distribution, and happy to run on hardware that other operating systems would shun for being underpowered, we can re-purpose any machine to become our server for no cost except time.

Linux comes in many forms, known as distributions, and it would be pointless to cover them all here, so we will consider two of the few popular ones: Debian and Ubuntu. Other distributions will perform just as well, so we should not consider this an exclusive list for our purposes.

Microsoft Windows

Microsoft Windows provides a perfectly good platform for running our server framework, and our components do not require a server edition of the underlying OS (although we may still require a server edition for licensing purposes). The instructions here are for Microsoft Windows Server 2003, but should work equally well on Microsoft Windows XP Professional Edition.

Which Version?

The following table shows the versions available for Linux and Microsoft Windows.

	Subversion	Apache	Trac
Current	1.4.5	2.2.6	0.10.4
Microsoft Windows	1.4.5	2.0.61	0.10.4
Linux Ubuntu 6.06 LTS	1.3.1	2.0.55	0.9.3
Linux Ubuntu 7.10	1.4.4	2.2.4	0.10.4
Linux Debian	1.4.2	2.2.3	0.10.3

It is obvious from the table above that there is a noticeable disparity in the versions available for the detailed platforms. Microsoft Windows has more flexibility than the other platforms in that it can easily run the latest version of all the components; however, as is apparent in the Appendices that cover installation steps, installation of the packages is far more easier on the other platforms.

Although we can use the latest/current versions of all the components on Linux, it is generally good practice to stick with packaged versions of software unless absolutely necessary. Therefore—with the exception of Trac itself—we will continue that practice. For Microsoft Windows we have no choice but to use packages directly from the relevant projects, with the exception of Apache. Since the development of Trac currently moves quicker than the packaging process on the Linux distributions concerned we will be manually installing it to ensure we have the most current version.

Time to Get Our Hands Dirty

Once we have chosen our server platform, it is time to get it working.

 This chapter mainly concerns configuration of our server machine. For both brevity and clarity, installation instructions are detailed in the appendices, to which you will be directed when needed.

Before we go any further, we need our foundations upon which to build. Now is the time to install the operating system of our choice on our server machine, ensure all the relevant security patches and updates are applied, and that we can access it from our client machine(s).

 Same destination, different paths

Although our configuration is *essentially* the same across both platforms, there can be different methods to achieve the end result, so where appropriate we will see specific instructions for each platform, and occasionally for individual Linux distributions.

Installing the Components

Now we should jump ahead to Appendices A, B, and C to follow platform-specific instructions to install Subversion, Apache, and Trac respectively. If you are using Microsoft Windows, you will have to install Apache first, then Subversion, and finally Trac. If Debian or Ubuntu is your preference, then we need to follow the instructions for Subversion and Trac, as the way in which the software is packaged on those platforms makes our life easier for us.

Following those instructions gave us our building blocks and now we can put them together.

Keeping It Organized

To make our lives easier, or for our system administrators, we need to keep the files for our projects together in a sensible fashion. To do this, we will first create a single folder—projects—and then create sub-folders for each component—svn, trac, and files for subversion, Trac, and WebDAV respectively—which will in turn hold the folders for our individual projects.

We will be setting up our directory structure based around our tools—each project will have a subdirectory under a folder for each component. We could approach it from the opposite direction and have a single directory per project with a folder for each component underneath, but this would create more administrative work as both Subversion and Trac can handle multiple projects nested in a single folder, but require manual configuration for multiple projects in multiple folders.

Before we go any further it is time to create some folders to store our Subversion and Trac repositories, and check that everything is working as expected. We're going to keep everything in the projects folder, which we will place in the root of the C: drive (Microsoft Windows) or the root partition (Linux).

The followings steps should be performed as a user with administrative rights from a command prompt (**Start** menu, **Run**, type cmd and click **OK**) for Microsoft Windows, or in a terminal as root, either directly (Debian) or via sudo (Ubuntu) for Linux.

1. For Microsoft Windows only, Type c: and press *Enter*.
2. Type cd \ (Microsoft Windows) or cd / (Linux) and press *Enter*.
3. Type mkdir projects and press *Enter*.
4. Type cd projects and press *Enter*.
5. Type mkdir svn trac files and press *Enter*.

Don't be afraid to personalize

Although we are creating our folders on our C: drive (Microsoft Windows) or in the root partition (Linux), this is only to keep things straightforward for this title. Feel free to place the projects folder wherever you feel appropriate on your own systems, but ensure you reflect such changes in the paths discussed in this chapter and the Appendices.

We will look at setting the file permissions for these folders correctly later in this chapter.

Customizing trac.cgi

This section is for Microsoft Windows only. We can safely ignore it if we are using Linux.

For Microsoft Windows we need to create a copy of the main Trac script and tweak it to use the version of Python we have installed.

1. Open a command prompt (**Start** menu, **Run**, type `cmd`, and click **OK**).

2. Type `copy "C:\Python24\share\trac\cgi-bin" "C:\Projects\"` and press *Enter*.

3. Type `exit` and press *Enter* to close your command prompt.

4. Open `C:\Projects\trac.cgi` in a text editor.

5. Change the first line to:

   `#!C:/Python24/python.exe`

6. Save and close the file.

Configuring Apache

Installation of our components is only part of the story, because we need to configure them to work together. We are using our web server Apache to provide — and control, as we will discover later — access to our components. At the moment it is only configured for typical web server activities, so we need to expand on that.

Virtual Hosts

Apache supports hosting multiple hosts or domains on a single server, a topic which is beyond the scope of this title. However, it may be useful to be aware that the components and configuration we are using here will work quite happily in such an environment. In fact such a configuration may help reduce hardware requirements by making a server multi-purpose.

Before we delve into configuration details, we need to know where to make our changes. Apache is controlled through a collection of configuration files that differ depending on the platform we are using. On Microsoft Windows the only file we really need to be concerned with is `httpd.conf`, which can be found in `C:\Program Files\Apache Group\Apache2\conf\`. Things are slightly more complicated under Linux as Debian and Ubuntu are configured to support virtual hosts out of the box, and configuration for individual hosts and modules is abstracted into individual files stored in `/etc/apache2/sites-available` and `/etc/apache2/mods-available` respectively. However, the simple presence of a file does not mean that it is recognized by Apache — they first have to be enabled. Fortunately — unless we chose to use virtual hosts — we need to enable only a couple of modules, and we can keep all our configuration in the file for the default host, which is unsurprisingly called `default`.

As already hinted, we need to make a few changes to the default Apache configuration. First of all we need to enable the `dav_fs` module, and then we need to append our configuration for dealing with serving multiple Trac projects and Subversion repositories, and also our WebDAV folders. Finally we will implement authentication mechanisms, although we will discuss the details of this later in this chapter.

Now we can tackle the much bigger task of configuring Apache to our requirements. Although this could be tackled as a whole, we are going to break it down into pieces so that we understand what each part does.

First we need to open the configuration file in a text editor ready to configure it. For Microsoft Windows this file is `C:\Program Files\Apache Group\Apache2\conf\httpd.conf` while for Ubuntu and Debian we will be using `/etc/apache2/sites-available/default`.

Enabling dav_fs

The instructions will diverge depending on the platform chosen.

For Microsoft Windows we need to edit our configuration file as follows:

1. Remove the leading comment marker (#) from line `164`.
2. Save the file.

For Ubuntu and Debian we need to execute the follow command as root:

1. `a2enmod dav_fs`

Both have the same result of enabling the `dav_fs` module.

Getting Apache to recognize our configuration changes

Apache reads its configuration files at startup and then ignores them. This means that we can change configuration settings while it is running, but we have to force it to use those changes. Although you can get it to reload the files, if you are making major changes the easiest way is to simply restart it.

Now we will append a series of sections to our configuration file. We can safely make all the changes in one go, but we will look at each set of changes individually so we can understand what they do.

First we will tell Apache that any and all requests for the (virtual) folder `projects` should be handled by Trac.

For Microsoft Windows:

```
ScriptAlias /projects C:/Projects/trac.cgi
```

For Linux:

```
ScriptAlias /projects /usr/share/trac/cgi-bin/trac.cgi
```

Next we will specify an environment variable that tells Trac that it is serving multiple projects and where to find those projects on the filesystem.

```
<Location "/projects">
    SetEnv TRAC_ENV_PARENT_DIR "/projects/trac"
</Location>
```

Trac supports two methods of authentication—HTTP and sessions. Authentication will be covered in more detail later in this chapter, but for now we need to know that we will be using HTTP authentication so that Apache can handle authentication to Trac, Subversion, and WebDAV for us.

First we will make sure that anyone accessing the login link within any project hosted on our server is required to be authenticated by Apache.

```
<LocationMatch "/projects/[^/]+/login">
    AuthType Basic
    AuthName "Trac Environment"
    AuthUserFile /projects/projects.passwd
    Require valid-user
</LocationMatch>
```

For Microsoft Windows the line `AuthUserFile` should be changed to:
`C:/Projects/projects.passwd`.

Now we will ensure that all access to Subversion via Apache is authenticated.

```
<Location /svn>
    DAV svn
    SVNParentPath /projects/svn
    AuthType Basic
    AuthName "Subversion Repositories"
    AuthUserFile /projects/projects.passwd
    Require valid-user
</Location>
```

As before `AuthUserFile` should be changed for Microsoft Windows. Additionally `SVNParentPath` should be changed to `C:/Projects/svn`.

Finally we can configure our `WebDAV` folder. This time we want all access to be authenticated except the viewing of files contained in either an `images` or `public` folder nested within our `WebDAV` folder (the method of retrieving a resource is known as GET in HTTP terms).

```
Alias /files /projects/files
<Location /files>
    DAV On
    AuthType Basic
    AuthName "Files"
    AuthUserFile /projects/projects.passwd
    Require valid-user
</Location>
<LocationMatch ^/files/[^/]+/(images|public)/>
    <LimitExcept GET OPTIONS>
        Require valid-user
    </LimitExcept>
</LocationMatch>
```

The same path changes made previously for Microsoft Windows will be needed in the above excerpt.

Now we can save our configuration file and restart Apache so that our changes will be recognized.

Creating Projects

Our server is configured to host our projects, but at the moment we don't have any projects to host! That is easily rectified though, so let's create ourselves a project to work on.

Every project needs a name, and our case it needs to be file system and URL friendly. If we stick to alphanumeric (letters—upper or lower case—and numbers) characters, hyphens, and underscores we should be fine.

For our test project we are going to be imaginative and call it 'sandbox'.

The followings steps should be performed as a user with administrative rights from a command prompt (**Start** menu, **Run**, type cmd and click **OK**) for Microsoft Windows, or in a terminal as root, either directly (Debian) or via sudo (Ubuntu) for Linux.

1. For Microsoft Windows only, Type c: and press *Enter.*

2. Type cd \Projects (Microsoft Windows) or cd /projects (Linux) and press *Enter.*

From here the commands are mostly the same across platforms. The only thing to watch out for is that Microsoft Windows expects backslashes in paths, while Linux expects forward slashes. The commands here — unless Microsoft Windows specific — will use forward slashes so we need to make sure we get the right type of slash when we type the commands.

1. Type svnadmin create svn/sandbox –fs-type fsfs and press Enter.

2. Type mkdir -p files/sandbox/public files/sandbox/private files/sandbox/images and press Enter.

3. Type \Python24\python.exe \Python24\Scripts\trac-admin (Microsoft Windows) or trac-admin (Linux) followed by trac/sandbox initenv and press Enter.

4. When prompted for a **Project Name** type Sandbox and press *Enter.*

5. When prompted for a **Database connection string** press *Enter* to accept the default.

6. When prompted for a **Repository type** press *Enter* to accept the default.

7. When prompted for a **Path to repository** type C:\Projects\svn\sandbox (Microsoft Windows) or /projects/svn/sandbox (Linux) and press *Enter.*

8. When prompted for a **Templates directory** press *Enter* to accept the default.

Following those commands will result in the following:

*   A Subversion repository
*   A folder structure within our WebDAV folder
*   A Trac environment (linked to the Subversion repository)

Now we can open up a web browser and point it to our server to see that everything is working.

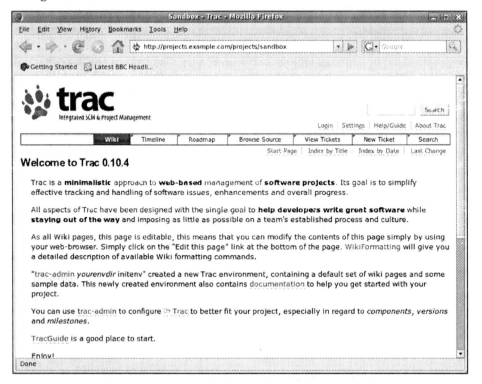

Security

At the moment our server is configured to allow access to certain actions — like writing to our subversion repository — only to authenticated users. Now we need to actually allow our users to perform these actions by storing their authentication details. These are stored in a text file that Apache understands — the `projects.passwd` file referred to in the earlier excerpts.

Managing Users

Creating this file is quite simple using the `htpasswd` tool provided by Apache, which should be accessible simply by its name on Linux or at `C:\Program Files\Apache Group\Apache2\bin\htpasswd.exe` for Microsoft Windows. We need to explicitly tell it to create a new file the first time, and which file to use for subsequent user additions.

For a first run, we use the following:

```
$ htpasswd -c /projects/projects.password joe
```

We will be prompted to specify and then confirm the password for our user joe. Alternatively we can specify the password as part of the command if we use the -b parameter, although we should be aware that this is not safe since the password will be stored in the command history of our Operating System.

For subsequent users we simply drop the -c:

```
$ htpasswd /projects/projects.passwd bob
```

Again we will have to specify and confirm bob's password. Now we have two users who can access our server.

Keeping in touch

With a minor configuration change, Trac is capable of sending emails when tickets are raised/updated. To make the most of this it is recommended that we use email addresses for our htpasswd usernames, then we need to do nothing besides enabling email.

See the **Notification** section of http://trac.edgewall.org/wiki/ TracIni to see how to enable this.

Editing or deleting users is simply a matter of modifying the password file. If we want to change their password we need to re-run the htpasswd command.

File Permissions

Since everything is running through Apache, we need to ensure it can write to the files it needs. Since we have put everything under the projects folder, we can set our permissions there and let them cascade down through the rest.

Linux

Linux file permissions are split into user, group, and other. We will change the group to the same one used by Apache, allow the group to write to our projects folder and then make sure the permissions are inherited by anything inside the folder.

As earlier, the following commands need to be performed by someone with administrative rights.

1. Type chgrp -R www-data /projects and press *Enter*.

2. Type chmod -R g+w /projects and press *Enter*.

3. Type chmod -R g+s /projects and press *Enter*.

Trac Permissions

Trac maintains it own set of permissions for each environment we create. The permissions we are going to create here cover the behavior described in the following chapters.

The default permissions in Trac allow unauthenticated (or rather anonymous) users to do anything. We are going to prevent them from editing the wiki — they can still view it though — and accessing the source code browser. Then we are going to let authenticated users do both of these as well as access milestones.

The followings steps should be performed as a user with administrative rights from a command prompt (**Start** menu, **Run**, type cmd and click **OK**) for Microsoft Windows, or in a terminal as root, either directly (Debian) or via sudo (Ubuntu) for Linux.

1. For Microsoft Windows only, Type **c:** and press *Enter*.

2. Type **cd \Projects** (Microsoft Windows) or **cd /projects** (Linux) and press *Enter*.

3. Type **\Python24\python.exe \Python24\Scripts\trac-admin** (Microsoft Windows) or **trac-admin** (Linux) followed by **trac/sandbox** and press *Enter*.

4. Type **permission remove anonymous WIKI_CREATE WIKI_MODIFY BROWSER_VIEW** and press *Enter*.

22. Type **permission add authenticated WIKI_ADMIN BROWSER_VIEW MILESTONE_ADMIN** and press *Enter*.

23. Type **quit** and press *Enter* to leave trac-admin.

Remember, we will need to do this for each Trac environment that we create.

Summary

In this chapter we looked at the various versions of the software available to us and discussed the choice of Operating System. After we installed and configured the software we created a home for our projects and created a sandbox environment to experiment in. We also looked at the various security-related tasks associated with our projects.

In the next chapter we will look at how to organize the files that we will be storing in our project.

4
Documentation

Documentation—if there is one word that instils fear in most developers, it must be this one. No one in their right mind would argue the value of documentation, but it is the actual act of writing it that concerns developers so.

As with everything else presented in the book, the secret of creating good documentation is to make the process of doing so as painless as possible, and if we are lucky maybe even attractive, to the developers. The only practical way to achieve that is to reduce friction. The last thing we need when we are in middle of fixing a bug is to wrestle with our word processor, or even worse try to find the right document to update.

What's in a name?

Throughout the rest of this chapter, and indeed the rest of this book, we will refer to various URLs that point to specific areas of our Trac environment, Subversion repository, or WebDAV folders. Whenever you see *servername*, replace it with your own server name.

Making Documentation Easy

One of the reasons Trac works so well for managing software development is because it is browser based. Apart from our development environment, the browser, along with our email client, are the next most likely applications we are going to have installed and running on our computer. If access to our Trac environment is only a click away, it stands to reason that we are more likely to use it.

In Chapter 2 we referred to Trac as a "wiki on steroids" because of the way the developers have integrated the typical features of a wiki throughout the whole product. However, for all the extra features and integration, at its heart Trac is basically just a wiki and this is the main reason why it so useful in helping smooth the documentation process. If we again recall Chapter 2, we described a wiki:

A wiki is a web application that allows visitors to create and modify its content.

Let's expand on that slightly. As well as letting us view content—like a normal website—a wiki lets us create or edit the content as we desire. This could take the form of creating new content, or simply touching up the spelling on something that already exists. While the general idea with a wiki is that anyone can edit them, in practice this can lead to abuse, vandalism, or spam. The obvious solution to this is to involve people to authenticate the edit, which we catered for when configuring our server in Chapter 3. We did this as part of setting the permissions for our Trac environment so that users are authenticated to carry out some activities, which in this instance specifically concerns creating and modifying content in our wiki.

Do we really need this security?

Yes. Having these security requirements provides us with accountability. We will always be able to see when something is done, but by enforcing security we can see who did it. While this does cause some administrative overhead to create and maintain authentication details for anyone involved with our development projects, the benefits outweigh the costs.

Accessing Trac

Before we look at how to modify and create pages, let's see how our Trac environment looks to a normal (i.e. unauthenticated) user. To do this we need to open our web browser and enter the URL `http://servername/projects/sandbox` into the address bar and then press the *Enter* key. This will take us to the default page (which is actually called WikiStart).

When we access our project as an unauthenticated (or anonymous in Trac parlance) user, the majority of it will look and act like a normal website and the wiki in particular seems just like the usual collection of interlinked pages.

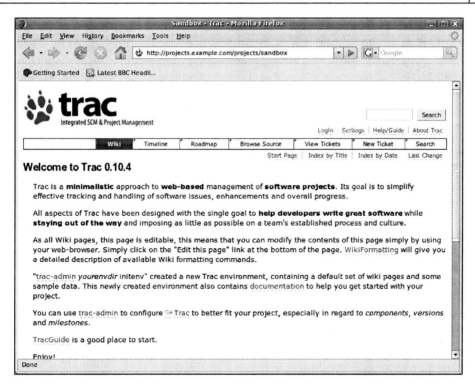

However, as soon as we authenticate ourselves to Apache (which passes that information on to Trac), it all changes.

If we click the **Login** link in the top right of the page now, we will be presented with our browser's usual authentication dialog box as shown in the following screenshot.

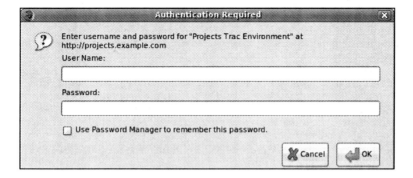

We need to put in the username and password we created for ourselves in Chapter 3 and click **OK**. If we enter them correctly we will be taken back to the same page, but this time there will be two differences.

Firstly, instead of the **login** link we will see the text **logged in as** followed by the username we used and a **Logout** link. Secondly, if we scroll to the bottom of the page there are some buttons that allow us to modify the page in various ways. Anonymous users have permission to only view wiki pages, while authenticated users have full control. We should try that out now—click the **Logout** link and scroll down again, and you will see that the buttons are absent.

A Touch of Style

Before we start editing the content in our wiki we should take some time to familiarize ourselves with the basics of the markup used by Trac. Since each Trac environment we create includes a copy of the Trac documentation in the wiki, this and other information is easy to find. Once we have logged back in, we need to click on the **WikiFormatting** link (or enter `http://servername/projects/sandbox/wiki/WikiFormatting` in the address bar of our browser).

The page describes the various ways in which we can format the text on our wiki pages, and contains both the markup and examples of how the text will be displayed. There is little need to repeat the whole of the page here, but we can have a look at some of the basic syntax before we move on.

Need to know basis

Instead of trying to absorb everything in one go, we will only look at the specific Trac markup when it is relevant to what we are discussing.

Formatting Text

The most commonly used text styles are bold, italics, and underlined. We can easily use these by wrapping the text we want to modify in specific characters as follows:

- Surrounding or 'wrapping', a word with three apostrophes will mark it as bold.

- Wrapping a word with two apostrophes will mark it as italicized.

- Wrapping a word with two underscore characters will make it underlined.

These don't just apply to individual words, we can wrap any amount of text in these markers or combine them.

Another common use of styles is to signify headings and sub-headings. This is done by wrapping a sentence with equals signs. The level of the heading is derived from the number of signs that surround the text.

E.g.

```
= This is the main heading =
This is some text.
== This is the sub-heading ==
=== This is a sub-sub-heading ===
== Another sub-heading ==
```

As a practical example, the title of this section as entered in a Trac wiki would be as follows:

```
== Formatting Text ==
```

The final important format is how to create links. As previously mentioned any CamelCase words will be automatically linked (for example the **WikiFormatting** link we clicked on the start page), as will raw URLs such as http://example.com. These types of links may be easy, but they do not look particularly nice. There is an alternative though. We can specify a link by wrapping two parts in square brackets ([]). The first part is the target for the link, and the second is the text that should be displayed. E.g.

```
[http://example.com some website]
```

We can also use the same format we use for linking to external sites to link pages within our wiki. We do this by using the wiki: prefix. E.g.

```
[wiki:SomePage some page]
```

Trac recognizes a variety of prefixes for linking to its different parts. As we are introduced to each part we will also learn the prefix we need to create links to it.

Preventing automatic links

Simply prefixing a CamelCased word with an exclamation mark (!) will prevent Trac from interpreting it as a wiki link. The exclamation mark will show up when editing and not while viewing the page.

Playtime

It's natural that we may want to try out our new-found knowledge of the wiki formatting rules and Trac makes that easy for us as well so we need not clutter our wiki with junk. If we enter `http://projects.example.com/projects/sandbox/wiki/SandBox` in our browser's address bar, we will be taken to the SandBox page within the wiki for our sandbox project (yes, we are being recursive). It is now different from any other wiki page, but it helps restrict our experiments to a single location. If we are logged in we should be able to see the **Edit this page** button. Go ahead and click it so we can see what it looks like when we edit a page.

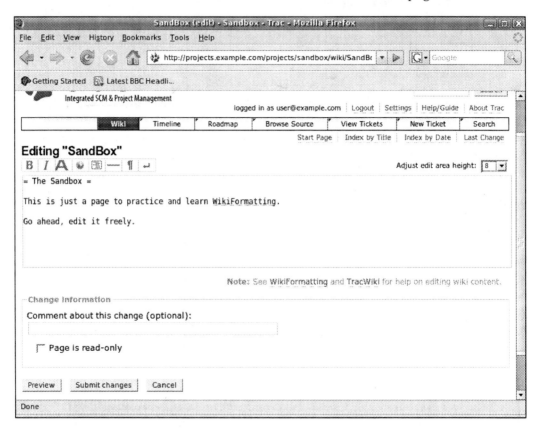

At the top we can see the formatting buttons that make editing a page more of a WYSIWYG (What You See Is What You Get) experience, along with a drop-down box that changes the size of the edit box. Next we have the edit box itself that contains the text and markup that makes the page we see when viewing it. Below this we have a comment box where we can provide a comment about the changes made and finally we have the buttons for submiting, previewing, or canceling our changes. We should make some changes to the contents of the page like so:

```
= The Sandbox =
This is just a page to practice and learn WikiFormatting.
Go ahead, edit it freely.
== My Changes ==
Wiki markup is ''so'' easy to '''use!'''
What about ThisPage?
```

Now if we hit the **Preview** button, we can see how our changes will be displayed. If we are not happy with them, we can scroll back up to our edit box and make the required changes. Now if someone else visits the page we are editing they will see the original. Only when we click the **Submit changes** button will the changes be stored.

Creating New Pages

If you were observant you will have noticed that our **ThisPage** link doesn't look like a normal link—it is gray and followed by a question mark (two actually, because we included one ourselves, but only one is part of the link). This is Trac telling us that although it recognised a wiki page, the page does not currently exist. However the link still works.

If we now click it we will be taken to an (almost) empty page with a **Create this page** button, which when clicked will take us to the edit view of a new page. Here, there is no difference between editing a new or an existing page.

Creating a link to a non-existent page is the easiest way to create new pages, but we can just as easily enter the name of a page in the address bar and get the same effect.

I can't find my page!

If we create a page that is not linked from any other pages, and we have forgotten what we called it we need not fear. Beneath the main Trac menu is a series of wiki-specific links. The second of these, **Index by Title**, will provide us with a list of all pages contained in the wiki.

Going Back in Time

Remember that we said that Trac has an internal version control system. Now we can explore to see how it works.

If we go back to the **SandBox** page, we should be able to see a **Last Change** link above the page contents. Clicking this will show us the changes made the last time the page was edited. We can see exactly what was added, removed, or modified.

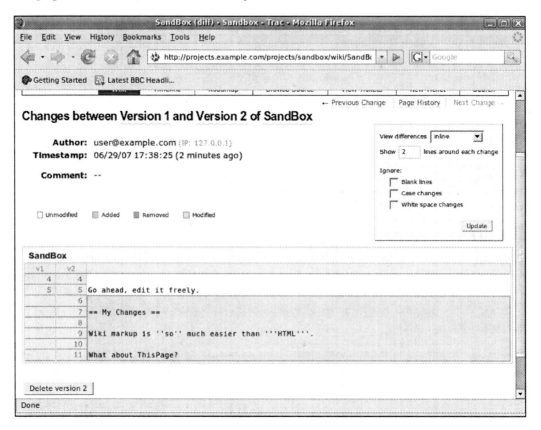

We can use the **Previous change** or **Next Change** links to navigate through the history of a page, or the **Page History** link to view the whole history in one go.

Taking It with Us

The final feature of Trac we are going to look at here is exporting. At the bottom of every page is a **Download in other formats** section, with links to the formats available. For the wiki the only (current) format is plain text, which is the raw text we see when editing a page. At first glance the usefulness of this feature may not be apparent; however, there is one area that can really benefit.

Most applications ship with some sort of plain text documentation, whether it is a version history, change log, or a basic 'read me' file. We can store and edit the contents of these files within our wiki, gaining all the benefits the wiki provides but we can still save them as plain text files when it is time to release.

Summary

In this chapter we have seen how Trac helps reduce the friction involved in creating documentation. We discovered the basics of formatting text and looked at how to edit and create new pages. In the next chapter we will continue our tour of Trac and in particular will see how to use tickets to track our development tasks.

5

Tracking Our Tasks

Back in Chapter 1 we looked at the basics of task management and how it could help us to manage our software development. There are many methods that can help us track our tasks, but the good news is that what we need for developing software is built right into Trac in the form of tickets.

Most developers, particularly those familiar with open-source projects, will be familiar with the concept of bug trackers. Typically, standalone systems allow users and developers alike to file bugs against the piece of software the tracker was set up to support. Once a bug has been reported, it needs to be assigned to someone—or someone takes ownership of it—who will be responsible for fixing it. People who have an interest in a particular bug can comment on it or subscribe to it so that they can be informed when it is fixed.

It should be obvious from the summary of bug trackers that they actually describe a development task; it is just that the scope is limited by the choice of language. For this reason Trac has tickets, and—by default—these can be categorized as **defects**, **enhancements**, or **tasks** to describe the different tasks we carry out during development.

First we will look at the sort of data tickets can contain and then at how we can customize them to suit our requirements. Next we will look at different ways of viewing the data collected through tickets. Finally we will look at how they can be used in conjunction with milestones to help us plan our project.

Tickets Please

The best way to familiarize ourselves with tickets is by creating one. When we set up our server we left it so that anyone could view, create, or modify tickets. However, we stay logged in while we create our first one.

To start creating our ticket, we simply need to click the **New Ticket** link in the main Trac menu.

Creating a ticket anonymously

Here we are creating a ticket while logged in, but when a ticket is created by someone who is not authenticated they will see an extra field at the top of form asking for their email address or username, which defaults to **Anonymous**.

The same form is used for creating or editing a ticket. The first field is **Short summary**. This is used to give the ticket a meaningful title, which will be useful later when we will look at ways of viewing tickets. This is followed by the ticket **Type**.

Next we have the **Full description**, which should be exactly that! — as much information as possible about the ticket. This field uses Trac's wiki engine, so we can use the markup we explored in Chapter 4.

We already know that CamelCased words are automatically turned into wiki links, and the same will happen here. We can also use the `wiki:` `SomePage` syntax to link to wiki pages from here. Trac will also recognize links to tickets. #1 will become a link to ticket number one, as will `ticket:1`. We can use these links anywhere in Trac that supports wiki formatting, so wiki pages can link to tickets and vice versa.

Then we have **Ticket Properties**, which fall into two groups — predetermined values and free text fields.

The fields that have predetermined values are as follows:

- **Priority**: Used to show the importance level of the ticket.
- **Component**: Used to show the part of the project to which the ticket belongs.
- **Milestone**: Used to show the particular milestone to which the ticket belongs.
- **Version**: Used to show the version of the project to which the ticket belongs

In a later section we will see how to change the values available for these fields.

The free text fields are as follows:

- **Keywords**: Used to make searching easier.
- **Assign To**: Used if the ticket has to be given to anyone in particular.
- **Cc**: Used to inform someone else about the ticket.

Finally we can indicate if we want to attach files to our ticket, and the ticket actions of previewing or submitting it. Except **Short summary** all the fields are optional, so let's add one now and leave the rest of the fields as they are and then hit **Submit ticket**.

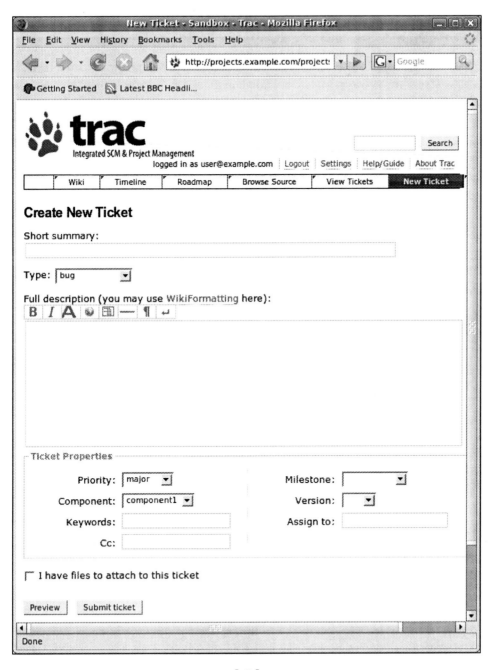

After the ticket has been stored we will be taken to the tickets page where we will be able to see the details we provided (or the default values where applicable) while creating the ticket. We will also have the option to attach files to our ticket.

The rest of the page is far more interesting though — we can use it to add comments to our ticket and change its properties. Let's try changing something now, like lowering the **Priority** from **major** to **minor**, and click **Submit changes**.

We're back at the same page again, but this time there is a **Change History** section that shows the change we made. This allows us to see the entire life cycle of a ticket at a glance.

The final part of the page is the **Action** section. This is where we indicate we are actually working on a ticket. We can choose to leave it in its current state, take ownership of it, mark it as resolved (with a variety of final statuses), or assign it to someone else by entering their email address.

Customization

When creating or editing a ticket there are five fields that have pre-determined values: **Type**, **Priority**, **Component**, **Milestone**, and **Version**. The values these fields can be chosen from can be changed by using the `trac-admin` tool.

The followings steps should be performed as a user with administrative rights from a command prompt (**Start** Menu, **Run**, type `cmd`, and click **OK**) for Microsoft Windows, or in a terminal as root, either directly (Debian) or via `sudo` (Ubuntu) for Linux.

1. Only for Microsoft Windows, Type `c:` and press *Enter.*
2. Type `cd \Projects` (Microsoft Windows) or `cd /projects` (Linux) and press *Enter.*
3. Type `\Python24\python.exe \Python24\Scripts\trac-admin` (Microsoft Windows) or `trac-admin` (Linux) followed by `trac/sandbox` and press *Enter.*

Ticket Types

Trac comes with three pre-defined ticket types. We can see the possible values with:

```
Trac [/projects/trac/sandbox] > ticket_type list
Possible Values
---------------
defect
enhancement
task
```

We can change an existing ticket type with:

```
ticket_type change <value> <newvalue>
```

E.g. to change defect to bug we would type:

```
ticket_type change defect bug
```

We can add a new type with:

```
ticket_type add <value>
```

Replacing add with remove will delete that type from the list.

Finally we can change the order with:

```
ticket_type order <value> up
```

This will move the specified value up the list. up can be replaced with down for obvious results.

Priority

 Priority is also known as severity within trac-admin.

Priority is used to indicate how important a ticket is to us. Similar to types, we can see the possible values with:

```
Trac [/projects/trac/sandbox]> priority list
Possible Values
---------------
blocker
critical
major
minor
trivial
```

As with types, the list can be edited with change, add, remove, and order commands.

In Chapter 1 we briefly discussed using priorities in task management, where we said that using them for task management was personal choice. If we choose to use them in out project, we should modify this list to reflect the priorities we have decided to use.

Component

Component is used to differentiate between different parts of a project. For example, we may have client and server components. We should customize the contents of this field to reflect the structure of our project.

As before, seeing the list of defined components is easy:

```
Trac [/projects/trac/sandbox] > component list
Name          Owner
--------------------
component1    somebody
component2    somebody
```

Unlike the last two though, components have an extra field—**Owner**. If we assign an owner to a component, and a ticket is marked as relating to that component then that ticket will be assigned to that person.

Components have the rename, add, remove, and chown commands. The first three behave similarly to the equivalent commands for the other fields, except that we can specify an owner when adding a component. The new chown command behaves like its UNIX namesake—it allows us to change ownership of a component, and takes two arguments: the name of the component and the new owner.

Milestone

We will look at milestones in more detail shortly, but for now we will see how to modify them.

 Unlike the rest of the fields, milestones can be managed directly through Trac.

Let's see what is already there:

```
Trac [/projects/trac/sandbox] > milestone list
Name          Due   Completed
-------------------------------
milestone1
milestone2
milestone3
milestone4
```

Milestones have a couple of additional attributes: the date they are due and the date they were completed. These are specified using the format YYYY-MM-DD.

As for the others we have the `rename`, `add`, and `remove` commands. When adding we can specify a due date in addition to the milestone name. There are also two new commands: `due` and `completed`, which allow us to set the respective attributes of a given milestone.

Version

The version field allows user to identify a particular release of our project. It could be argued that **Version** and **Milestone** provide the same functionality, which to a degree is true. However the distinction is: we work toward milestones, while a version marks where we have been. Another way of looking at it is that a given ticket describes a defect in version *x* which we are planning to fix in milestone *y*.

As with components and milestones, the default list is pretty unimaginative:

```
Trac [/projects/trac/sandbox]> version list
Name    Time
----------
2.0
1.0
```

Like milestones we can assign a date to a version, which we should think of as the release date.

The usual commands show up here with `rename`, `add`, and `remove` being supplemented by `time`, which behaves much like `due` and `completed` do for milestones.

Customizing Default Values

When a ticket is created, most fields have a default value. Like the pre-determined fields though, we can customize this. Default values are controlled by the file `/projects/trac/<projectname>/conf/trac.ini`. In that file there is a ticket section as follows:

```
[ticket]
default_component =
default_milestone =
default_priority = major
default_type = defect
default_version =
restrict_owner = false
```

If we change this section, the next ticket created after we have saved it will reflect the changes.

Viewing Tickets

Although we have already seen what a ticket looks like when we view it directly, we are yet to explore the ticket reporting capabilities of Trac. If we click the **View Tickets** link in Trac's main menu, we will be taken to the list of default reports. Clicking on any one of these reports will provide us with the summary information of each ticket that matches the report's filter.

The list of default reports should suffice for most requirements, but if they do not we have a custom query builder available so we can write our own. This can be found just under the main Trac menu when viewing reports. We can use this builder to create complex queries and view the results on the fly.

At the moment Trac doesn't support saving custom queries, but it does come close. We can link to queries in two ways from anywhere in Trac that supports wiki formatting (even other tickets!).

Linked Queries

These use the same formatting as normal links within a wiki, but this time they start with the `query:` designator. We can either craft the query link by hand using Trac's query language, or more easily simply grab the query from the address bar in our browser.

For example, a query that has the URL of `http://projects.example.com/projects/sandbox/query?type=bug&order=priority` can be expressed as linked query as follows:

```
query:?type=bug&order=priority
```

Embedded Queries

By using the TicketQuery macro, we can embed a list of tickets anywhere that supports wiki formatting.

What is a macro?

A macro is a small program or script that, in the case of Trac, alters the content of the wiki. Examples include automatically creating a table of contents for a page, inserting a date/time or inserting a list of tickets. There is a default set of macros distributed with Trac, and we can obtain more from: `http://trac.edgewall.org/wiki/MacroBazaar`.

To include the same data as opposite directly in a page, we would use the following:

```
[[TicketQuery(type=bug&order=priority)]]
```

When the page is viewed, we would see a list of ticket IDs and their summaries.

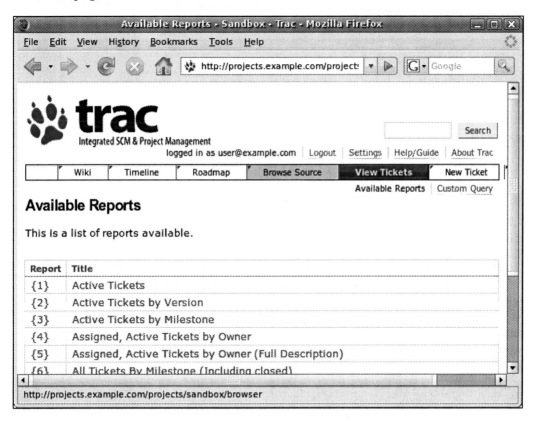

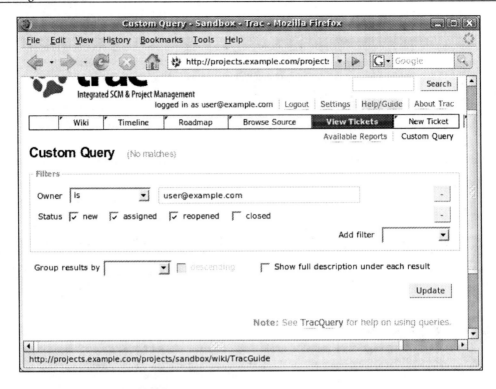

Using Milestones

Milestones allow us to group tickets together and then track our progress toward meeting that milestone based on whether tickets have been resolved or not. When all tickets associated with a milestone have been resolved, then that milestone should be considered met.

We have already seen how to create milestones through the admin application, and we know we can associate tickets with them from a given ticket's page. We access milestones via the Roadmap view, which is available through the **Roadmap** button on the main menu. This will give us an overview of unmet milestones and their progress. If we are logged in, we will also see the option to add a new milestone.

 See Chapter 3 for details on the security we configured in our Trac instance.

Clicking on the name of a milestone will show us detailed information, including a breakdown of progress by component or other ticket fields. It will also give us the option to edit or delete the milestone.

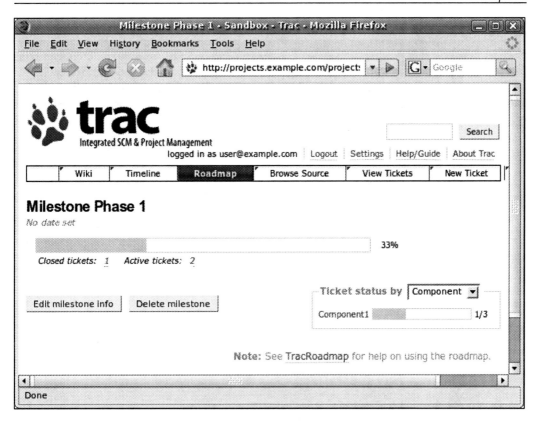

When creating or editing a milestone we can specify its name, due and completed dates, and a description. We currently cannot set the description through the admin interface, but can only do so through Trac. Hopefully this will be addressed in a future release. The description supports wiki formatting.

 It should come as no surprise now that Trac can link to milestones as well as queries, tickets, and wiki pages. We need to use the `milestone:` prefix to indicate that it is a link to a milestone.

Using milestones to group our tickets together allows us an instant view of progress and, if we are using components, where to focus our efforts to meet our targets.

Summary

In this chapter we explored the fields that make up tickets in Trac, how to customize them to suit our needs, and how to report on our tickets so that we can manage them effectively. Now that we are familiar with tickets, in the next chapter we will take a look at Subversion—how to use it to separate our development efforts, and finally how it integrates with Trac through the source code browser.

6

Version Control 101

Although we will do our planning and project (task) management within Trac, the title is concerned with managing software development, which actually includes developing something. We can't (yet) develop software in a wiki—no matter how good it is! Therefore it's time now to leave the safe—and now hopefully familiar—confines of Trac and look elsewhere. One of the benefits of Trac is that it doesn't care what our software is or what we are using to develop it. The only thing that matters is that the code is stored in a Version Control System—specifically Subversion.

You say to-mato, I say tom-ato...

When reading about Subversion we will see that it is often interchanged with svn, which is the command we run to use it. We should feel free to use the pronunciation we are most comfortable with—anyone else who uses it should recognize and acknowledge both.

We will cover what you need to know for using the system and processes described in this title and then move on to branching and merging—techniques that allow us to isolate our changes during development.

Check Out, Check In

In Chapter 3 we set up our Subversion repository. This currently exists only on our project server. Although we can perform some basic actions directly on this (as we will see shortly), to actually use Subversion we need to have a **working copy** of this on our client machine. We can get this working copy by performing an action known as **checking out**. Once we have made some changes to our working copy we will **check them in** to the repository. Until we check in our changes they are not a part of the version history in our repository.

Currently our repository is completely empty, and ideally we need to define a basic structure to keep things organized later. We could make these changes on our working copy, but instead we'll make them directly in our repository.

First we will ensure that subversion works and we can access our server from our client.

We need to perform the following steps from a command prompt (**Start** menu, **Run**, type cmd, and click **OK**) for Microsoft Windows, or in a terminal on our client machine. No special privileges are required.

1. For Microsoft Windows only, Type `c:` and press *Enter*.
2. Type `cd \` (Microsoft Windows) or `cd` (Linux) and press *Enter*.
3. Type `mkdir projects` and press *Enter*.
4. Type `cd projects` and press *Enter*.

This is were be will store our working copies once we start using them. Note that on Microsoft Windows we are creating this folder in the root of the `c:` drive, while we are creating it under our home directory on Linux. We can store this folder anywhere we like on our client machines.

1. Type `svn info http://servername/svn/sandbox` and press *Enter*.

We should be prompted for authentication to access our repository — these are the same details we used to log into Trac. We will first be prompted to authenticate with our current username. Entering a blank password will result in us being asked for our username and password. Once we have authenticated with a given repository, we should not be asked to do so on the same computer as the same user (from an Operating System perspective). An example of a successful authentication and the subsequent command output is shown below.

```
$ svn info http://projects.example.com/svn/sandboxAuthentication
realm: <http://projects.example.com:80> Subversion Repositories
Password for 'jdoe':
Authentication realm: <http://projects.example.com:80> Subversion
Repositories
Username: user@example.com
Password for 'user@example.com':
Path: sandbox
URL: http://projects.example.com/svn/sandbox
Repository Root: http://projects.example.com/svn/sandbox
Repository UUID: 677246c4-9c0b-4019-ac6e-f268985e4c37
Revision: 0
Node Kind: directory
Last Changed Rev: 0
Last Changed Date: 2007-05-13 17:32:38 +0100 (Sun, 13 May 2007)
```

The highlighted lines show where we were prompted to authenticate, and that the repository has no version information stored in it.

If we run the command again, we should not be prompted for authentication.

Having determined that everything is working, we can now create our initial repository structure. Best practices within the Subversion community prescribe that each repository (that hosts a single project, as ours does) have three folders at its root: trunk, tags, and branches. trunk is considered the mainline of the development and it is this folder that our working copy will really be of; tags are used to mark specific moments in time (e.g. milestones and releases), while branches will be explored later in this chapter. Technically there is no difference between a tag and branch in Subversion; it is just convention (mainly from its predecessor CVS) that require these to be separate. Our initial working copy will come from the trunk folder.

As we have already discussed we could check out our repositories, create the folders, and commit the changes, and this is a perfectly valid approach. Instead we will create them directly in the repository and then check out the trunk folder.

2. Type:

```
svn mkdir http://servername/svn/sandbox/trunk
                http://servername/svn/sandbox/tags
                http://servername/svn/sandbox/branches
                -m "Initial repository structure"
```
and then press *Enter*.

The -m "Initial repository structure" specifies a log message for the action(s) we are performing—creating folders in this fashion is actually checking in the changes directly on the server. Later we will look at manually specifying these messages.

Before we check out the trunk, let's have another look at the repository information:

```
$ svn info http://projects.example.com/svn/sandbox
Path: sandbox
URL: http://projects.example.com/svn/sandbox
Repository Root: http://projects.example.com/svn/sandbox
Repository UUID: 677246c4-9c0b-4019-ac6e-f268985e4c37
Revision: 1
Node Kind: directory
Last Changed Author: user@example.com
Last Changed Rev: 1
Last Changed Date: 2007-08-11 14:01:20 +0100 (Sat, 11 Aug 2007)
```

The highlighted text shows that the Revision number of the repository has increased by one.

Now we can check out a copy of the `trunk`.

3. Type:
   `svn checkout http://servername/svn/sandbox/trunk sandbox`
   and press *Enter*.

This will check out a copy of the `trunk` into a folder called `sandbox` (which we are storing in our local projects folder).

Too much typing

By the end of this chapter we will be sick of typing long Subversion commands. Fortunately it supports shortcuts for some commands, for e.g. co for `checkout` and ci for `checkin`. Run svn `help` to see a list of available commands and their shortcuts (shown in parentheses).

After Subversion has told us which revision we have checked out (Revision 1 in this case), we can run the information command against our working copy.

4. Type **cd sandbox** and press *Enter*.

5. Type **svn info** and press *Enter*.

```
$ svn info
Path: .
URL: http://projects.example.com/svn/sandbox/trunk
Repository Root: http://projects.example.com/svn/sandbox
Repository UUID: 677246c4-9c0b-4019-ac6e-f268985e4c37
Revision: 1
Node Kind: directory
Schedule: normal
Last Changed Author: user@example.com
Last Changed Rev: 1
Last Changed Date: 2007-08-11 14:01:20 +0100 (Sat, 11 Aug 2007)
```

Notice that we did not have to supply a URL for the information command this time. This is because Subversion knows when it is in a folder under revision control due to the hidden `.svn` folders containing its information. Try it out—run `svn info` in another (uncontrolled) folder and see what happens.

Numeric values do not take quotation marks while string values do. But, when using the map notation, quotation marks are not required for property names if they are written in camel-cased DOM notation.

Now we have our working copy of the trunk, we can make some changes. We should create a single or several files in our local sandbox folder. In the following examples some simple Python scripts will be used for our files. When we have done that, we need to let Subversion know about them—until we do so, they will not be under version control. To see what has been changed since the last revision, we can use the `status` command.

6. Type **svn status** and press *Enter.*

    ```
    $ svn status
    ?       foo.py
    ```

The ? indicates that the file is unknown to subversion. To correct this we will add the file.

7. Type **svn add foo.py** and press *Enter.*

    ```
    $ svn add foo.py
    A       foo.py
    ```

Now our file is marked with an A, which tells us the file has been added. Reviewing the `status` again will provide the same listing. Subversion uses a number of character codes to represent a file or folder's status, some of which are shown below. For more information on the possible codes, run `svn help status`.

Code	Meaning
?	Not under version control
A	Added, but not yet checked in
M	Modified
<blank>	Unmodified
I	Ignored by Subversion
!	Missing

Although we have added our file to Subversion, it is not yet under version control. So to achieve this we have to **check in** or **commit** our changes—that will store them in our repositories.

8. Type **svn commit** and press *Enter.*

Since we did not specify a log message (the -m parameter) we will be prompted to provide one using a temporary file in our default text editor. We need to add our log entry ("Created sample script.") and save the file. As the Subversion commit action progresses we will receive details of what is happening.

```
$ svn commit
Adding            foo.py
Transmitting file data .
Committed revision 2.
```

If we run the info command again on our working copy and the repository we will see that something is wrong! The repository is indeed on revision 2, but our working copy is still on revision 1. How did that happen? The reason is that our working copy is just a copy. commit commands work directly on the repository as we saw earlier. Resynchronizing our working copy with the repository is easy with the update command.

9. Type **svn update** and press *Enter*.

The next command we will see is very useful, although of course it could be argued that they are all useful. The command in question is log, which allows us to see the history of a repository or even a specific file or folder within it.

10. Type **svn log** and press *Enter*.

```
$ svn log
------------------------------------------------------------------------
r2 | user@example.com | 2007-08-12 14:26:46 +0100 (Sun, 12 Aug 2007) |
3 lines

Created sample script.

------------------------------------------------------------------------
r1 | user@example.com | 2007-08-11 14:01:20 +0100 (Sat, 11 Aug 2007) |
1 line

Initial repository structure
------------------------------------------------------------------------
```

Make another change to the file and check in the changes, then see how the info and log have changed.

What's the Difference?

Apart from allowing us to travel through time for any file under its control, Subversion can also tell us exactly what changed between versions or the changes we made to our working copy. If we make some changes to our one-and-only project file, but don't check them in, we can look at how this works.

First we can see what has changed in our working copy compared to the latest version (known as 'head').

1. Type **svn status** and press *Enter*.

```
$ svn status
M       foo.py
```

From the previous table above we can tell that foo.py has been modified. We can see what changes have been made to that file with the diff command.

2. Type **svn diff foo.py** and press *Enter*.

```
$ svn diff foo.py
Index: foo.py
===================================================================
--- foo.py      (revision 3)
+++ foo.py      (working copy)
@@ -1,4 +1,3 @@
 #! /usr/bin/python
-print "Hello, world!"
 name = raw_input('What is your name? ')
 print 'Hello, %s' % name
```

Subversion defaults to displaying its differences using the unified diff format, which is understood by a wide variety of tools. We can also understand it with a little practice. The two lines after the header tell us about the files that are being compared, in this case the head and work copy versions of the file. The symbols before the filenames describe the prefix the output will use to indicate the file a particular line belongs to. Lines that are same in both files have no prefix.

Using this basic understanding, we can determine that the line -print "Hello, world!" is present only in the head copy of the file, meaning we have deleted it from the working copy.

Changing your mind

If you decide the changes made to the working copy are not good and you want to go back to the previous version, you can achieve it with the `revert` command: `svn revert foo.py`

Spotting lines that have been added or removed is easy, but what about lines that have been changed?

```
$ svn diff foo.py
Index: foo.py
===================================================================
--- foo.py      (revision 3)
+++ foo.py      (working copy)
@@ -1,4 +1,4 @@
 #! /usr/bin/python
-print "Hello, world!"
+print "Hello, World!"
 name = raw_input('What is your name? ')
 print 'Hello, %s' % name
```

In this case we are shown the same line from both the files; we can see the line that was removed and the line that it was replaced with.

A whole new line?

`diff` deal with files on a line-by-line basis, so even if only one character has been changed — as above — it considers that the whole line as being changed.

We can also perform a `diff` on different versions of a file in the repository. To see what changed between the last two revisions of our file perform the following:

3. Type **svn diff -r 2:3 foo.py** and press *Enter*.

```
$ svn diff -r 2:3 foo.py
Index: foo.py
===================================================================
--- foo.py      (revision 2)
+++ foo.py      (revision 3)
@@ -1,2 +1,4 @@
 #! /usr/bin/python
 print "Hello, world!"
+name = raw_input('What is your name? ')
+print 'Hello, %s' % name
```

Easy on the Eyes

Although the log and diff output that Subversion provides is perfectly adequate for working with it, there is a better way—especially for sharing between team members. It's time to return to Trac and explore its code browser.

Where is it?

When we set up our security in Chapter 3 we restricted the code browser to authenticated users, so we need log in (if we are not already logged in) before we can continue. See Chapter 4 for a refresher on how to do this.

We need to click the **Browse Source** link in the main Trac menu to see the default view, which is the latest version of the root of our repository. If we click on **trunk** we will see the contents of that folder, and clicking on the file name will show the latest version of that file along with some of the meta-information Subversion stores. If instead of clicking on the file name we click on the version number beside it, we will be shown the Subversion log for that file. Finally by clicking on a Changeset number within the log we will be able to see what was changed for that revision. If we just want to see the most recent change, we can click the **Last Change** link in the default view.

Linking to code

Like the other features of Trac, we can link to parts of the code browser in areas that support wiki formatting. We can link to changesets, files, revisions of files, differences between files, and other views. All the ways of doing these are detailed in the wiki page TracLinks, which exists in every Trac environment we configure.

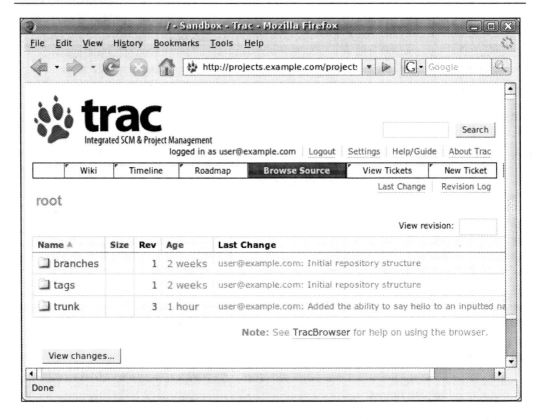

Opening a New Branch

We have seen how Subversion allows us to keep our code under control as we develop; now we will see how we can use it to develop *safely*.

Consider this series of events: we spend a few days perfecting new reporting functionality for our application, but it depends on an already existing function. While we are writing our code another developer changes the way the function works, which causes our code to break, and checks that in. We then check our code in, without realizing that it no longer works. The end result? The code in trunk is **broken**. This is a situation we should strive to avoid—ideally the code in trunk should always work (undiscovered/unresolved bugs not withstanding).

So how do we develop things and get the benefits of Subversion if we can't check in incomplete code? The answer is by using branches.

When to check in?

This is purely a personal preference, but most will say that we should only check in code that works. This can result in large gaps between checkins, so we can counter that by breaking large changes into smaller ones. This is not a hard and fast rule though, so be prepared to adapt when required.

A branch is quite simply a copy of a folder in the repository. We create a branch for the feature or bug we are working on, checking in as we go. Once we have completed that section we will then **merge** our changes back into the trunk. There is a caveat though—our branch will be based on a moment in time, and the trunk may change between the creation of our branch and when we merge our changes back in. We need to take responsibility for ensuring our changes merge cleanly with other changes that may have been made.

Creating a branch is quite simple, but we need to make the changes in the repository rather than our working copy.

1. Type:

    ```
    svn copy http://servername/svn/sandbox/trunk http://servername
        /svn/sandbox/branches/mybranch -m "Created a branch"
    ```
    and press *Enter*.

As with any other change to the repository, this results in the revision number being incremented—revisions are repository-wide.

We now have two choices for working with our branch: we can check it out into another folder, or we can `switch` our current working copy to use it. Since we already know how to do the former, we'll try out the latter.

2. Type `svn switch http://servername/svn/sandbox/branches/mybranch` and press *Enter*.

We can confirm the switch has happened by using the `info` command again. Any changes we make and commit will now be stored in our branch rather than the trunk. Go ahead and make some.

To switch or check out?

A good approach is to maintain two working copies of a project's trunk, which we will call stable and unstable. We will never touch the stable other than to update it or run/test the code. All changes are made in the unstable copy, which we can either recreate every time we work on a new branch or use switch to change to the branch we want.

This approach pays dividends when we are working with larger projects where we may want to branch only a single folder or work with multiple (non-conflicting) branches.

When we have finished our changes—and checked them in!—we need to merge them back into the trunk. First we need to switch our working copy back to the `trunk`.

3. Type `svn switch http://servername/svn/sandbox/trunk` and press *Enter*.

Now we need to determine which revisions we want to merge into the trunk.

4. Type:

   `svn log http://servername/svn/sandbox/branches/`
   `mybranch --stop-on-copy`
   and press *Enter*.

This provides us with the log entries for our branch from the point it was created up to its latest change.

```
$ svn log http://projects.example.com/svn/sandbox/branches/mybranch -
-stop-on-copy
------------------------------------------------------------------------
r5 | user@example.com | 2007-08-22 12:58:33 +0100 (Wed, 22 Aug 2007) |
1 line

Made greeting more polite
------------------------------------------------------------------------
r4 | user@example.com | 2007-08-22 12:52:57 +0100 (Wed, 22 Aug 2007) |
1 line

Created a branch
------------------------------------------------------------------------
```

From this we can see that we want to merge all changes between revision 4 and 5 (not a very complex branch).

5. Type:

   `svn merge -r4:5 http://servername/svn/sandbox/branches/mybranch`
   and press *Enter*.

We now have the changes from our branch, but we need to check them in.

6. Type `svn ci -m "Merged changes from mybranch"` and press *Enter*.

Finally, if we no longer require our branch, we can clean up by deleting our branch. Don't worry though—we can always get it back later. This is a good habit to get into, as we will see in the next chapter.

7. Type:
    `svn delete http://servername/svn/sandbox/branches/mybranch -m`
    `"Removing obsolete branch"` and press *Enter*.

Summary

This brings us to the end of our introduction to the various tools. In the next chapter we will see how they can be used together to manage various stages in a project's life cycle.

7
Putting It All Together

In the last few chapters we looked at various Trac features and learned the basics of Subversion. We will now put all this together and see how using our solution can help us manage software development.

We will look at the two specific activities that are repeated most often during the software development process — implementing a new feature and fixing a bug — and follow the work flow through each of them.

Our Feature Presentation

One popular way to view an application is as a collection of features. What are features? Features allow our application to be useful, or may even be its reason for existing. Consider the ubiquitous text editor — a pretty simple application at first glance. It not only lets us edit text, but also open, save, and print files. Of course features can have sub-features; text editing will also include things like cut, copy, and paste, spell check, formatting, etc.

Thinking of an application in terms of features (sub-features, and sub-sub-features) allows us to break down our projects into chunks or tasks, which are much easier to manage. Of course some features will be inter-dependent, but we should consider them independent and move to the next one only when one has been completed. If the feature we want to work on depends on another feature, then we need to complete that feature. Refer back to Chapter 1 and see how thinking in terms of features fits well into our introduction to task management — tasks and features are one and the same thing.

Creepy Crawlies

Bugs, (yet another) bane of a developer's life. They can manifest in the strangest ways that make finding and fixing them extremely hard. Every developer has to deal with bugs as no code is perfect. Bugs can be caused by the platform rather than the code written. Like features, bugs should be considered standalone and addressed in isolation from other changes, unless there are obvious dependencies. This approach not only brings the obvious task management benefits, but is also less likely to introduce more bugs if we keep our changes in focus.

Is There Any Difference?

The short answer is no. Besides the obvious difference in how features requests and bugs are initially reported, the only other significant difference is that features are generally new code while bugs almost exclusively deal with existing code.

A Common Sequence

As we have just seen, our two sequences are actually quite similar. Both require *something* to be reported — either a feature request or a bug, which in Trac terminology are an **enhancement** and a **defect** respectively. However both are types of ticket, and tickets equate to tasks, which is what we are aiming to manage.

> **Tasks and tasks**
>
> When we first looked at tickets in Chapter 5, we saw that defect, enhancement, and task were default ticket types. We also use the term task in relation to project management. Fortunately we can safely avoid confusing the two — we will not be using the task ticket type in this chapter.

Once we have our ticket and we have decided that this is something we are going to tackle, then we move on to the execution of that task, and finally mark the task as complete by resolving the ticket. Here is the sequence of events, including the steps required to execute the task:

1. Raise a ticket.
2. Target to a milestone.
3. Assign to a developer.
4. Create a branch.
5. Make the changes.
6. Merge into the trunk.
7. Resolve the ticket.

Although we use the same sequence of events for both features and bugs, the details for each are sufficiently different and we only want to deal with an overview here.

 One benefit of using tickets to track tasks is that we get a numerical reference — the ticket number — which can be used in branch names and commit logs to keep everything together.

Adding a Feature

Features could come in from many sources, but ideally they should be controlled by the development team or — if they are lucky enough to have one — their development manager. Features may be suggested by users, requested by customers, or created by the developers themselves. Ultimately three decisions need to be made about each proposed feature: **if**, **when**, and **who**. None of these really need much explanation beyond what we have already covered in Chapter 1. However, **if** is worth touching on again. Not every feature should make the cut when deciding what is going to be included in our project. There are no absolute rules for this, but if we generally ask the question whether or not a feature should be included in our application, then the answer should be no. Of course this does not stop people from requesting features!

By now we should think of tickets and milestones within Trac, but we do not need a ticket for every feature. Instead, features should start out in the wiki. We need a page, for e.g. **ProposedFeatures**, which would lists the proposed features along with a summary for each and optionally have a separate page for those features that require more detailed information or discussion. Since it is a wiki page, anyone with access can modify this list, or features can be fleshed out in their own pages before they are added to the list. Our development team can then review this list when planning our next set of milestones and the features we intend to include in each of them. As features make or miss the cut, they can be amended with links to the relevant tickets or moved to another page e.g. **PlannedFeatures**. By using the wiki and its versioning features we now have no excuse for losing sight of a feature once it has been proposed. We should also use the same list to keep track of feature requests that come in via tickets, perhaps using the ticket query macros as shown in Chapter 5.

Now having decided that we are actually going to implement a particular feature or not — our **if** question — it is time to raise a ticket. We may already have one if that was how the feature was proposed. We won't repeat what we have seen previously, but we will look at certain aspects of the process. For explicit details for the steps discussed here, refer to Chapter 5.

The most obvious thing is that feature requests should have the **enhancement** ticket type. The description of the ticket can be copied from our features wiki page, or if the feature has its own page we can link to it. If we have defined **components** for our project then we should select the right one either now or in the next step.

Once we have raised our ticket, we need to decide **when**, and for that we use the milestone feature of Trac. If we do not have a relevant milestone configured, then we should do that now. We can then modify our ticket to choose the milestone we are targeting.

 Unfortunately, Trac currently does not have the concept of ticket dependencies so this is something we need to manage ourselves using the wiki formatting to provide links between related tickets.

We now have a list of features that need to be implemented, and thanks to our milestones we know which we should be working on now. We can see these in the following two ways:

1. Via the Roadmap view, accessed from the **Roadmap** entry on the menu bar in Trac.

2. Via the **View Tickets** entry on the menu bar and then choosing the **Active Tickets by Milestone** report.

Having raised our ticket and decided when we are going to do it, we need to decide **who** will implement it. We do this by assigning the ticket to someone, who then becomes responsible for executing any actions required by the ticket, including closing it when complete. This is also known as resolving the ticket. We do this by editing the ticket and either accepting it — if we are going to perform the work — or assigning it to a valid user name of someone in our development team.

Once tickets have been assigned to someone they can easily view their tickets via the **View Tickets** entry on the menu bar and then choosing the **My Tickets** report. Now our developers have a simple job of working through the open tickets on their list.

As already discussed, each ticket should have its own branch. We do this so that changes made are isolated from the development trunk and from other branches. This means that we are always developing against a known quantity — the trunk. Our branches are created exactly as shown in the previous chapter, except that the branch name and commit log should make a reference to the ticket number, e.g. for ticket #29 we could call our branch `feature-29` or `feature-29-add_spell_checking` and our commit log would be something like `"Branched to add spell checking. See ticket #29."`. As we are developing something new, our branch should be made from the `HEAD` revision of the trunk.

Now we can finally do what we do best — develop — safe in the knowledge that:

1. We know exactly what we are supposed to be doing.
2. What we are doing is not going to affect anyone else until we merge.

Since we are working in our own branch, we can **commit** our changes as often as we like and we should take advantage of this. The only rule is that we have to commit prior to **merging** the changes back into the trunk. The decision to merge should be based on one question only: *is the feature complete?* If the answer is positive, we should stop coding, commit and merge. We should not be tempted to overdevelop a feature or re-use a branch — once we have merged into the trunk and committed the changes, then the branch should be discarded or even deleted. As with the branch log, the merge log should make reference to the feature ticket number e.g. `"Addresses ticket #29 by implementing spell checking."`.

What about code reviews?

Code reviews are a good thing, and if we do not have them in place already then we should. We should integrate them into the processes described in this book wherever we feel they are appropriate.

Once our changes have been merged into the trunk, our ticket can be marked as resolved, and to close the loop within Trac, a comment should be added, which makes reference to the revision that resulted from the merge. Using comments in this way means that we can used the interlinking feature of Trac to link our ticket to the revision in the Subversion that contains the changes. We can view this revision through the code browser in Trac; and by including the ticket number in our commit log in Subversion, a link will be created between the revision in the code browser and the tickets that drove the changes.

Now our code is merged and our ticket resolved. Our feature is now complete and our milestone is a step closer. Now it's time to start on the next one.

Tagging a Release

When we have completed all the features and bugs for a milestone it is time to release. This will consist of actions like testing, quality assurance, packaging, and distribution, but here we are only concerned with one: tagging. This allows us to capture a snapshot of our Subversion repository at that moment in time that is subsequently easy to return to. We could just work with revision numbers and remember each one for future reference, but tags make the process friendly and give a feeling of accomplishment. Without tags the code will seem in a constant state of flux, whereas with them we have solid points of reference.

Creating a tag has the same process as branching, which was described in Chapter 6, except that we place them in the `tags` path rather than `branches`. Tag names should correspond to the milestones we have defined in Trac.

Fixing a Bug

We need to follow a slightly different work flow for fixing a bug. Bugs—or defects in Trac terminology—should always start with a ticket, even if it is one of the developers who discovers it. New bugs should be processed on a regular basis—an activity commonly referred to as **triage**—with the frequency being anything from the moment each bug is reported to hourly, daily, or even weekly but we should not have a processing cycle longer than that. This process aims to answer a few immediate questions:

- Has it been reported before?
- Is the report valid?
- Is it reproducible?
- How severe is it?

Different projects may have different questions, but if we can answer these then we have a good start. The benefit of asking the first question is obvious: if a ticket for a similar bug already exists we can resolve this one as a **duplicate** within Trac and move on. We should remember, though, to add a comment saying which ticket this is a duplicate of. If this is genuinely a new bug then we need to establish whether the ticket contains enough information to proceed or not. If not then we may need to enter into a dialog with the reporter to obtain more information. Determining whether a bug is reproducible also saves us time—if the bug only manifests itself for the reporter then our developer will have a harder time trying to fix it. Lastly deciding how severe the bug is lets us prioritize our bugs, and again Trac provides a mechanism for this through the **severity** field within tickets.

Once we have a triaged bug then we need to ask the same **if, when,** and **who** questions as we did for a feature. Although we like to fix every single bug, the simple reality is that we cannot. First we need to decide if we are going to fix it, a decision most likely based on how severe it is and whether we can reproduce it. Trac provides us with the **wontfix** resolution for tickets that we are never going to address. For the bugs we are going to address, we should now target them to milestones just as we did for features. Here the secret is to be realistic about the bugs we are going to address in each milestone—if we assign all to the next milestone we will never reach it. Severe bugs have a higher priority and so should be targeted earlier, but we should not just address high priority bugs. Finally we can assign the bug to a developer to actually fix.

Now our process relates more clearly with the one for features. However, branching for bugs is slightly different. Since we are dealing with code that already exists we will probably not want to branch from the HEAD revision of the trunk, but rather an earlier revision. Finding the right revision can be an issue, but we have already seen the solution for this—tags. As bugs are generally filed against a particular version or milestone of our application, then being able to branch from the relevant tag makes life much easier. As before our branch name and log should reference the ticket number, e.g. for ticket #51 we could call our branch `bug-51` and our commit log would be something like `"Branched to fix ticket #51 - Crashes when saving."`.

We can now use our branch to find and fix the bug. Determining exactly how to fix a bug is not always obvious, and once again Trac helps us with this. Tickets can be used to track the dialog relating to that ticket, and we can use this along with the code browser to obtain help from other developers in our team to pinpoint the cause and find a solution. Once we have fixed it we can merge our changes back into the trunk—referencing the ticket once more—and then resolve our ticket as before.

Summary

In this chapter we saw how to address the two most common tasks during a software development project—adding a feature and fixing a bug. We not only saw the common work flow shared by these two activities but also how they differ. We looked at how to plan work using milestones and use tags in Subversion to mark significant moments in time—like the completion of our milestones.

With our knowledge of project management for software development, our project server using Trac and Subversion, and the skills and processes for using them to add features and fix bugs, we are now ready to manage our software development.

Installing Subversion

This appendix covers detailed, step-by-step instructions for installing Subversion on your system, and covers Microsoft Windows and Linux. Unless otherwise noted, these instructions apply to both Client and Server installations.

Microsoft Windows

 If you are configuring a server, you should install Apache (Appendix B) prior to installing Subversion.

1. Download and run `svn-1.4.5-setup.exe` from `http://subversion.tigris.org/files/documents/15/39559/svn-1.4.5-setup.exe`. You should observe the following screenshot:

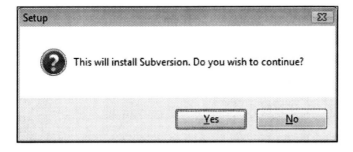

 Although this book is using the latest version available at the time of writing, times do change and software always gets updated. To get the latest version of Subversion, visit:

`http://subversion.tigris.org/servlets/ProjectDocumentList?folderID=91`

2. Click **Yes** and then **Next** to progress and pass the welcome screen.

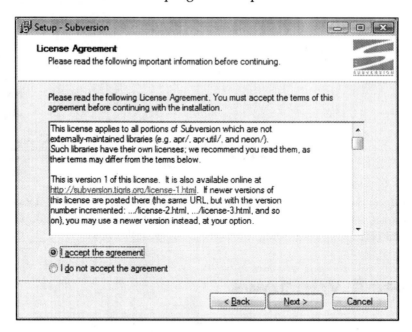

3. Select **I accept the agreement** and click **Next**.

4. Click **Next**.

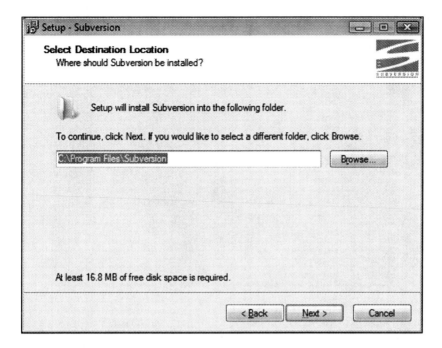

5. Change the installation path if required (not recommended) and click **Next**.

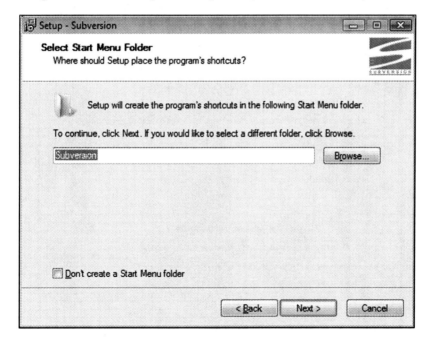

6. Change the folder name if required (not recommended) and click **Next**.

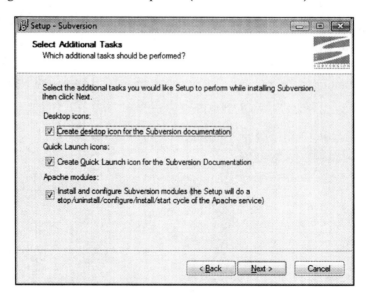

 If you have not installed Apache, the final option **Install and configure Subversion modules** will not be shown.

7. Deselect the **Desktop icons** and **Quick Launch icons** options, but leave the **Apache modules** option selected and click **Next**.

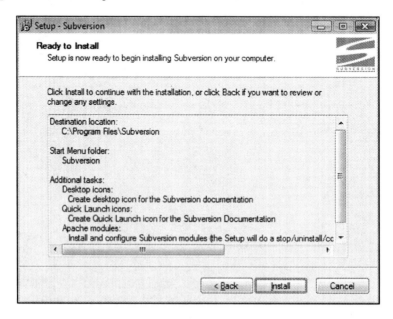

8. Confirm the details and click **Install**.

9. Wait while the installation takes place.

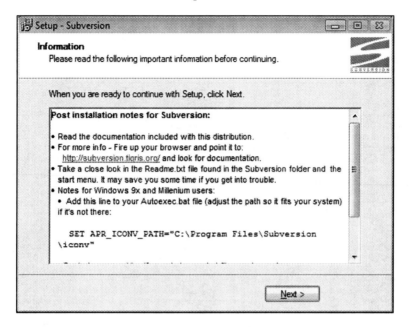

10. Click **Next**.

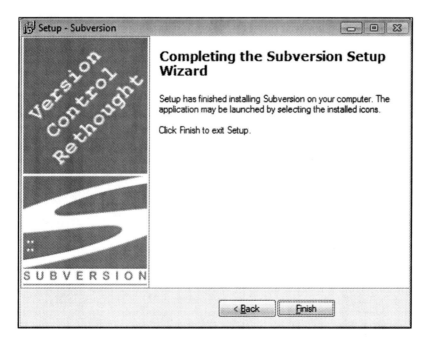

11. Click **Finish**.

You can test the installation by opening a command prompt and typing
`svn --version` then pressing *Enter*. If everything is working OK we should see a
result similar to the following (most of the output will have flowed off the screen):

```
Command Prompt                                                    _ □ x
C:\Users\Dave>svn --version
svn, version 1.4.5 (r25188)
   compiled Aug 22 2007, 20:49:04

Copyright (C) 2000-2006 CollabNet.
Subversion is open source software, see http://subversion.tigris.org/
This product includes software developed by CollabNet (http://www.Collab.Net/).

The following repository access (RA) modules are available:

* ra_dav : Module for accessing a repository via WebDAV (DeltaV) protocol.
  - handles 'http' scheme
  - handles 'https' scheme
* ra_svn : Module for accessing a repository using the svn network protocol.
  - handles 'svn' scheme
* ra_local : Module for accessing a repository on local disk.
  - handles 'file' scheme

C:\Users\Dave>_
```

Linux

We will discuss Ubuntu and Debian in the following section.

Ubuntu and Debian

Things are much easier under Ubuntu and Debian. To install Subversion simply use
the following instructions.

Client

To install Subversion on your client, use the following command from the console:

```
$ sudo apt-get install subversion
```

Answer **yes** when are asked to confirm the action, and that is it!

Server

Installing the server components under Linux is significantly easier than on Microsoft Windows. Use the following command from the console:

```
$ sudo apt-get install subversion libapache2-svn
```

Again answer yes when prompted. This will automatically install Subversion, Apache, and the Apache Subversion module for us all in one go.

B

Installing Apache

This appendix covers detailed, step-by-step instructions for installing the Apache web server on your system, and covers Microsoft Windows and Linux. Apache is needed only on the Server side, not on the Client.

Specific configuration of Apache for the solution described in this book is covered in Chapter 3.

Microsoft Windows

For Server installations on Microsoft Windows, Apache should be installed before installing Subversion. Doing so means that the Subversion installs will detect the presence of Apache and will automatically configure itself accordingly. In simpler terms, doing it this way means less work.

Although this book is using the latest version available at the time of writing, times do change and software always gets updated. To get the latest version of Apache, visit:

http://www.mirrorservice.org/sites/ftp.apache.org/httpd/binaries/win32/

or

http://httpd.apache.org/download.cgi

1. Download and run `apache_2.0.61-win32-x86-no_ssl.msi` from `http://www.mirrorservice.org/sites/ftp.apache.org/httpd/ binaries/win32/apache_2.0.61-win32-x86-no_ssl.msi`. The following window will be observed:

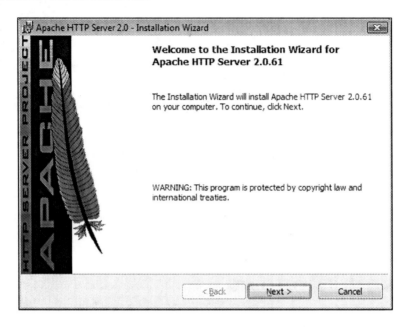

2. Click **Next**.

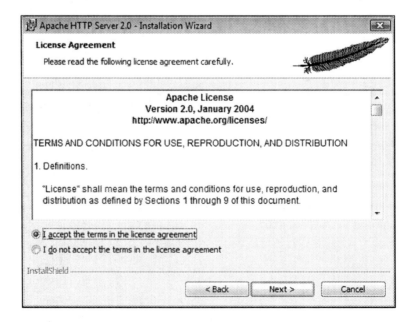

3. Select **I accept the terms in the license agreement** and click **Next**.

4. Click **Next**.

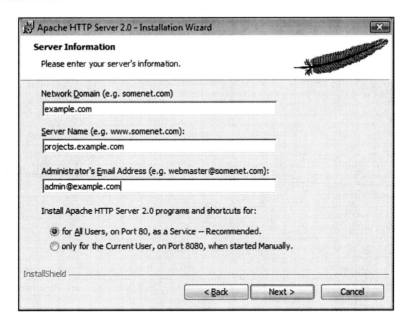

5. Change the **Network Domain, Server Name**, and **Administrator's Email Address** as required and click **Next**.

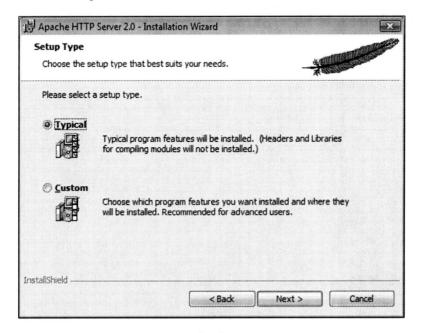

6. Click **Next** to accept the **Typical** installation.

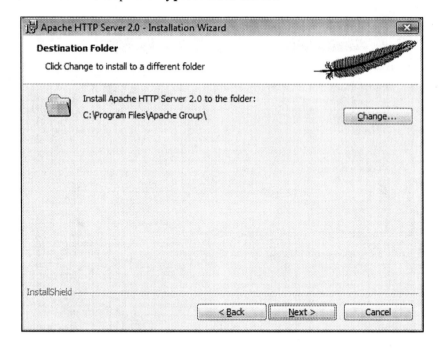

7. Change the installation folder if required (not recommended) and click **Next**.

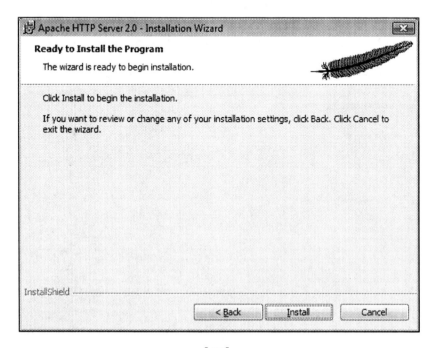

8. Click **Install** to start the installation.

9. Wait while the installation takes place.

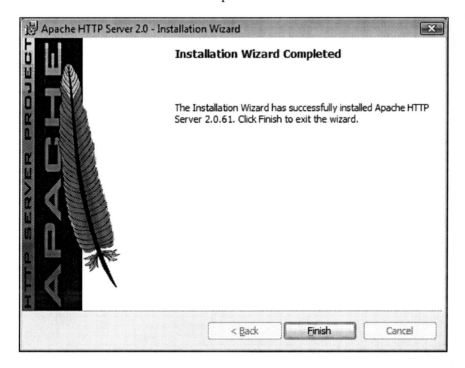

10. Click **Finish** to complete the installation.

Linux

We will discuss Ubuntu and Debian in the following section.

Ubuntu and Debian

Installation of Apache is far easier under Ubuntu and Debian as the package management software used will handle the dependencies for us.

To install Apache, simply run the following command from a console:

```
$ sudo apt-get install apache2
```

Answer **yes** when prompted.

However this will only install Apache. We need to have Apache and Subversion installed on our server. See Appendix A for details of installing Subversion.

C

Installing Trac

This appendix covers detailed, step-by-step instructions for installing Trac and its dependencies, and covers Microsoft Windows and Linux. Trac needs to be installed on your server. You will use a web browser to access it from other machines.

Trac is very easy to install, but has a number of dependencies that must be satisfied first. As Trac is written in Python, our first requirement is obvious. There are several versions of Python available, but the recommended version is 2.4. For data storage Trac can use a variety of databases. SQLite was the only original option, and remains the most popular, primarily because it is the easiest to configure. For these reasons the instructions that follow assume you will also use SQLite.

Keeping your options open

Although these instructions cover only SQLite, you can choose a different database if you wish. Details of using alternatives can be found at:

`http://trac.edgewall.org/wiki/DatabaseBackend`

SQLite is unusual in that there is no server software to install. Instead databases are single files, which can be used by any application that uses the SQLite library. This means that for Trac, we need to have the Python SQLite library installed. In order to communicate with Subversion, Trac requires the Python Subversion library. Finally it uses ClearSilver for its template system.

Future Proofing

Although Trac uses ClearSilver in the version covered by this book (0.10.x), the developers have replaced it with a different system called Genshi for the version currently in development (0.11). Details on Genshi can be found at:

`http://genshi.edgewall.org/`

Microsoft Windows

The following section describes the required installations.

Python

1. Download and run `python-2.4.4.msi` from `http://www.python.org/ftp/python/2.4.4/python-2.4.4.msi`. The following window will be observed.

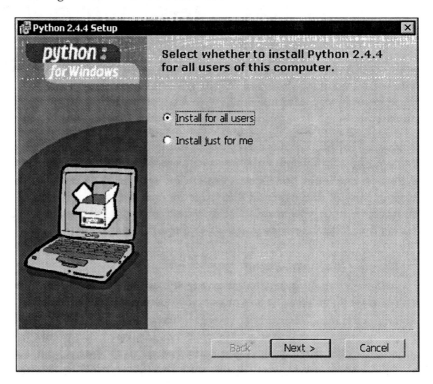

 Although this book is using the latest version available at the time of writing, times do change and software always gets updated. To get the latest version of Python 2.4, visit:

`http://www.python.org/download/`

2. Leave **Install for all users** selected and click **Next**.

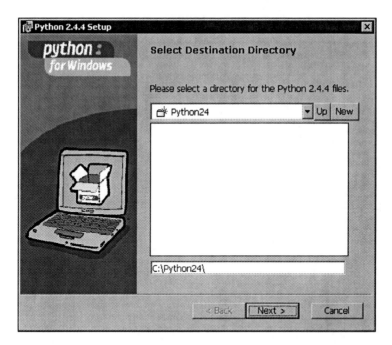

3. Click **Next** to accept the default destination directory.

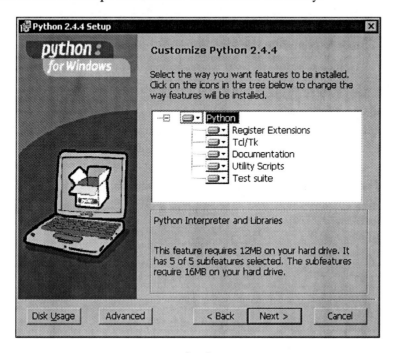

4. Leave all features selected and click **Next**.

5. Wait while the installation takes place.

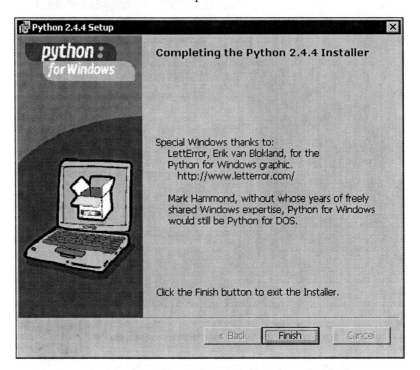

6. Click **Finish** to complete the installation.

Python Subversion Bindings

1. Download and run svn-python-1.4.4.win32-py2.4.exe from
   `http://subversion.tigris.org/files/documents/15/38214/`
   `svn-python-1.4.4.win32-py2.4.exe`.

 The latest version of this package can be found at:
`http://subversion.tigris.org/servlets/ProjectDocumentL`
`ist?folderID=91`

2. Click **Next** to skip the welcome screen.

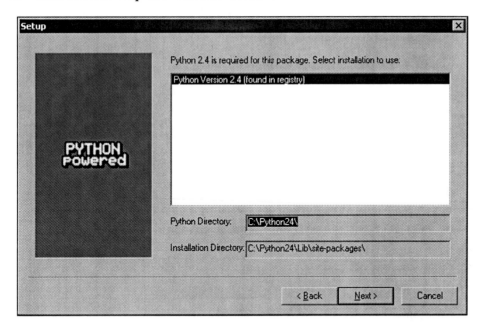

3. Ensure that Python 2.4 is selected and click **Next**.

Potential for confusion

It is possible to have multiple versions of Python installed side-by-side. If this is the case for you, then in the previous step you need to ensure the correct version (2.4) is chosen.

4. Click **Next** to start the installation.
5. Click **Finish** to complete the installation.

Python SQLite Bindings

1. Download and run pysqlite-2.3.5.win32-py2.4.exe from
    `http://initd.org/pub/software/pysqlite/releases/2.3/2.3.5/`
    `pysqlite-2.3.5.win32-py2.4.exe`.

To obtain the latest version (again, making sure it is for Python 2.4) visit:

`http://www.initd.org/tracker/pysqlite/wiki/pysqlite`

2. Click **Next** to skip past the welcome screen.

3. Ensure Python 2.4 is selected and click **Next**.

4. Click **Next** to start the installation.

5. Click **Finish** to complete the installation.

ClearSilver

1. Download and run clearsilver-0.9.14.win32-py2.4.exe from `http://www.clearsilver.net/downloads/win32/clearsilver-0.9.14.win32-py2.4.exe`.

 To obtain the latest version of ClearSilver for Python 2.4, visit:

`http://www.clearsilver.net/downloads/`

2. Click **Next** on the welcome screen.

3. Ensure Python 2.4 is selected and click **Next**.

4. Click **Next** to start the installation.

5. Click **Finish** to complete the installation.

Trac

1. Download and run trac-0.10.4.win32.exe from `http://ftp.edgewall.com/pub/trac/trac-0.10.4.win32.exe`.

 To obtain the latest version of Trac, visit:

`http://trac.edgewall.org/wiki/TracDownload`

2. Click **Next** at the welcome screen.

3. Ensure Python 2.4 is selected and click **Next**.

4. Click **Next** to start the installation.

5. Click **Finish** to complete the installation.

Linux

Installing Trac under Linux requires us to carry out the same two steps as for Microsoft Windows—installing the dependencies, and installing Trac itself.

Ubuntu and Debian

Installing the Dependencies

These can be installed with the following command:

```
$ sudo apt-get install python2.4-pysqlite2 python2.4-subversion
                       python-clearsilver
```

Installing Trac

1. Download Trac with:
   `wget http://ftp.edgewall.com/pub/trac/trac-0.10.4.tar.gz`

2. Extract the files with:
   `tar -xzf trac-0.10.4.tar.gz`

3. Change into the extracted folder with:
   `cd trac-0.10.4`

4. Run the installation with:
   `sudo python setup.py install`

Index

U

Ubuntu and Debain, Linux
  Apache, installing 93
  dependencies, installing 101
  Subversion, installing on client 86
  Subversion, installing on server 87
  Trac, installing 101

W

WebDAV
  about 22
  uses 22
wiki, Trac
  about 38
  content, editing 40
  page history 44
  plain text files, exporting 45
  SandBox, edting 42, 43
  text, formatting 40, 41

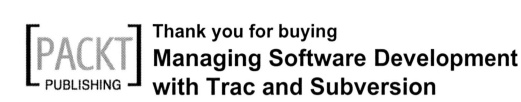

Thank you for buying
Managing Software Development with Trac and Subversion

Packt Open Source Project Royalties

When we sell a book written on an Open Source project, we pay a royalty directly to that project. Therefore by purchasing Managing Software Development with Trac and Subversion, Packt will have given some of the money received to the Trac project and Subversion project.

In the long term, we see ourselves and you—customers and readers of our books—as part of the Open Source ecosystem, providing sustainable revenue for the projects we publish on. Our aim at Packt is to establish publishing royalties as an essential part of the service and support a business model that sustains Open Source.

If you're working with an Open Source project that you would like us to publish on, and subsequently pay royalties to, please get in touch with us.

Writing for Packt

We welcome all inquiries from people who are interested in authoring. Book proposals should be sent to authors@packtpub.com. If your book idea is still at an early stage and you would like to discuss it first before writing a formal book proposal, contact us; one of our commissioning editors will get in touch with you.

We're not just looking for published authors; if you have strong technical skills but no writing experience, our experienced editors can help you develop a writing career, or simply get some additional reward for your expertise.

About Packt Publishing

Packt, pronounced 'packed', published its first book "Mastering phpMyAdmin for Effective MySQL Management" in April 2004 and subsequently continued to specialize in publishing highly focused books on specific technologies and solutions.

Our books and publications share the experiences of your fellow IT professionals in adapting and customizing today's systems, applications, and frameworks. Our solution-based books give you the knowledge and power to customize the software and technologies you're using to get the job done. Packt books are more specific and less general than the IT books you have seen in the past. Our unique business model allows us to bring you more focused information, giving you more of what you need to know, and less of what you don't.

Packt is a modern, yet unique publishing company, which focuses on producing quality, cutting-edge books for communities of developers, administrators, and newbies alike. For more information, please visit our website: www.PacktPub.com.

Ruby on Rails Enterprise Application Development

ISBN: 978-1-847190-85-7   Paperback: 400 pages

Building a complete Ruby on Rails business application from start to finish

1. Create a non-trivial, business-focused Rails application

2. Solve the real-world problems of developing and deploying Rails applications in a business environment

3. Apply the principles behind Rails development to practical real-world situations

Linux Thin Client Networks Design and Deployment

ISBN: 978-1-847192-04-2   Paperback: 180 pages

A quick guide for System Administrators

1. Learn to implement the right Linux thin client network for your requirements

2. Evaluate and choose the right hardware and software for your deployment

3. Techniques to intelligently design and set up your thin client networkt

4. Practical advice on educating users, convincing management, and intelligent use of legacy systems

Please check **www.PacktPub.com** for information on our titles

CherryPy Essentials

ISBN: 978-1-904811-84-8   Paperback: 272 pages

Design, develop, test, and deploy your Python web applications easily

1. Walks through building a complete Python web application using CherryPy 3

2. The CherryPy HTTP:Python interface

3. Use CherryPy with other Python libraries

4. Design, security, testing, and deployment

Managing eZ Publish Web Content Management Projects

ISBN: 978-1-847191-72-4   Paperback: 270 pages

Strategies, best practices, and techniques for implementing eZ publish open-source CMS projects to delight your clients

1. Tips and expert advice for the whole eZ publish web CMS project lifecycle

2. Learn about the requirements and success factors of an eZ project

3. Implement eZ publish projects successfully, efficiently, and effectively

Please check **www.PacktPub.com** for information on our titles

Printed in the United Kingdom
by Lightning Source UK Ltd.
126001UK00001B/146/A